USING THE POTTER'S WHEEL

USING THE POTTER'S WHEEL

DONALD CAMPBELL

PHOTOGRAPHS BY ADRIENNE CAMPBELL

VAN NOSTRAND REINHOLD COMPANY
New York Cincinnati Toronto London Melbourne

This book is dedicated to Karl Martz and Berenice Abbott.

Copyright © 1978 by Litton Educational Publishing, Inc.
Library of Congress Catalog Card Number 77-28398
ISBN 0-442-21461-8

Printed in United States of America.
Designed by Adrienne Campbell.

Published in 1978 by Van Nostrand Reinhold Company
A division of Litton Educational Publishing, Inc.
135 West 50th Street, New York, NY 10020, U.S.A.

Van Nostrand Reinhold Limited
1410 Birchmount Road
Scarborough, Ontario MIP 2E7, Canada

Van Nostrand Reinhold Australia Pty. Ltd.
17 Queen Street
Mitcham, Victoria 3132, Australia

Van Nostrand Reinhold Company Limited
Molly Millars Lane
Wokingham, Berkshire, England

Library of Congress Cataloging in Publication Data

Campbell, Donald
    Using the potter's wheel.

    Includes index.
    1. Pottery craft.   I. Title.
TT920.C35   738.1'42   77-28398
ISBN 0-442-21461-8

CONTENTS

INTRODUCTION

The potter's wheel has been in use for more than five thousand years, appearing first in the Middle East and soon after in many other parts of the world. Although refinements have changed its appearance and increased its efficiency, it remains essentially a very simple device. As used today, it may be bare-bones plain; sleek, mechanized, and rather expensive; or, yet again, so primitive as to suggest some unevolved counterpart from the dim reaches of the Bronze Age.

While most of the important tools and processes of pottery making have been written about extensively, the potter's wheel and its capabilities have been slighted. One always gets a smattering of them in general texts—enough to whet the appetite and make one wish for a more extensive treatment. This book attempts to remedy that circumstance. A manual of photographs with accompanying text, it shows the most basic kinds of forms that can be made on the wheel as well as the methods utilized later in trimming and drying them. Though wheel-thrown cylinders, spheres, and cones are often used today in making pure sculptures, the purpose here is to show and describe the making of utilitarian forms—or pots, as potters would call them.

While the advice the commentary offers is for the most part simple, direct, and in the public domain of craftsmanship and commonsense, it is not meant to shut off experiment or establish a body of dogma that cannot be contradicted. On the contrary, each person must discover for himself the precise hand and body positions, the pressures against the clay, and the wheel speeds that will enable him to work comfortably and naturally. Five potters will have five ways to center, lift, and shape; and ten will have ten. But all of these ways will have in common some basic principles.

Watching a potter throw on the wheel is somewhat like listening to a pianist perform at the keyboard. One hears a rhythmic cascade of sound and is probably unaware of the hours spent in gaining the finger and wrist dexterity needed to play beautiful trills and octaves. Or one sees a ball of clay effortlessly pulled into a fluid form and is equally unaware of the time spent in learning to control a widening curve and keep the clay spinning on center. Before either artist can make music, aural or visual, a set of basic technical problems must be solved.

Those confronting the potter at the wheel are explained carefully in this book.

A beginner will not suddenly become an accomplished potter after reading these pages. That will take many pleasant, frustrating hours throwing pots and most likely some study with a teacher who can criticize shortcomings and suggest ways to overcome them. Nevertheless the book's value is real. In addition to what was claimed for it above—the description of basic forms and the presentation of fundamental concepts—it will enable the student to compare his methods of working to those in the visual checklist which the photographs provide.

Reading and viewing the book from beginning to end is the most beneficial way to use it, not necessarily due to the material's increasing difficulty—although that frequently is true—but rather because later sections occasionally omit photographs of key sequences which have been previously shown and described in detail.

Unless the sense of the situation or the picture captions indicate otherwise, it should be assumed when looking at the photographs that the wheel is spinning.

Perhaps most readers of this book already have access to a wheel, either their own or one in a school or a shop. However, for those who are considering the purchase of a wheel, there is a listing in the Appendix of representative kinds which are available. One should become acquainted with key specifications and, in addition, take into consideration shipping expense and warranty information as well as one's own special requirements—for example, the amount of space one has available for the wheel, the quantity of clay and the size of the pots one will be working with, the frequency with which the wheel will be used, etc. A wheel that at the time of purchase barely satisfies one's minimum requirements is usually a poor investment; there is little opportunity for growth and development. Before making a decision, try to get as much first-hand information as possible. Talk to studio potters and teachers of ceramics. Their experience and advice can be valuable.

1/BASICS

WEDGING

To center and throw on the wheel, the potter must have a ball of clay that is entirely free of lumps and air pockets. This homogeneity is given to the clay by a kneading process called wedging. There are several wedging techniques that work satisfactorily. Three are shown here. Try all of them to see which one you prefer.

It is not possible to say exactly how long or how many times you should wedge the clay. The heat of the hands and the absorbency of the surface on which you are wedging may actually dry the clay too much if it is

1. A chunk of plastic clay is cut into halves by a taut wire that is mounted on the wedging board.

2. Throw one half onto the board and slam the other piece on top of it. Throw hard so that no air pockets are trapped beneath the halves.

3. Again cut through the clay with the wire, but make this cut at a right angle to that of the first one.

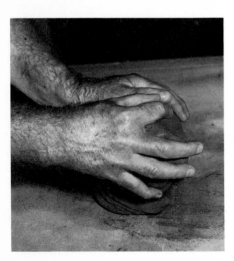

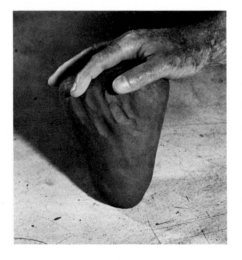

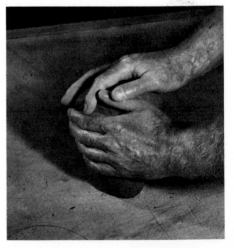

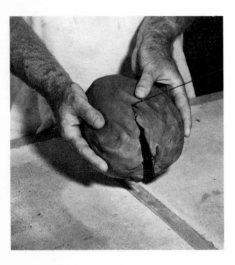

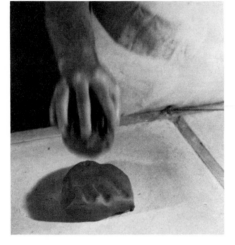

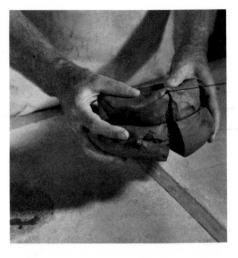

7. This end view shows the clay being rolled. The wrists bend backward; the heels of the palms push into the mass; the clay starts wrapping around itself. Repeat 50–100 times.

8. A third technique provides the best wedging method (although the one most difficult to master—and to photograph). The clay is formed in a conical shape and tilted up on its point.

9. With the right hand covering the base of the cone, as in the previous photograph, the left hand is placed along the side of the form. The fingers are in contact with each other.

kneaded excessively. Although it is pointless to wedge longer than necessary, the proof of the wedging is in the throwing. If your clay at the wheel is lumpy and filled with air, you should modify the method that you are using. Perhaps you must wedge longer.

Wedge at a table whose height is comfortable. The surface should be flat and somewhat absorbent so that the clay does not stick to it. A table top covered with canvas makes a good wedging board as does a heavy slab of plaster. You can easily make a small

drying/wedging board by constructing a two-foot-square, 1-by-4-inch frame, with a 3/4-inch plywood bottom, and filling it with plaster of paris. The mixing of plaster is described in the Appendix.

As you work, you will soon collect wheel trimmings, which should be soaked, and quantities of heavy, liquid clay, called slip. These will need to be reconditioned. They can be spread out thinly on a plaster slab whose absòrbency will begin to dry them. Later, the clay can be wedged and used again.

4. The halves are smashed together again. By repeating the cutting and slamming steps several dozen times, clays of different consistency and type can be brought to near homogeneity.

5. With a second technique satisfactory wedging can be given to the clay if it is kneaded somewhat like a piece of dough. Grasp a piece of clay around the left side.

6. Place the right hand around the other end. Keep pressing the hands together as the clay is rolled so the form does not elongate into a coil.

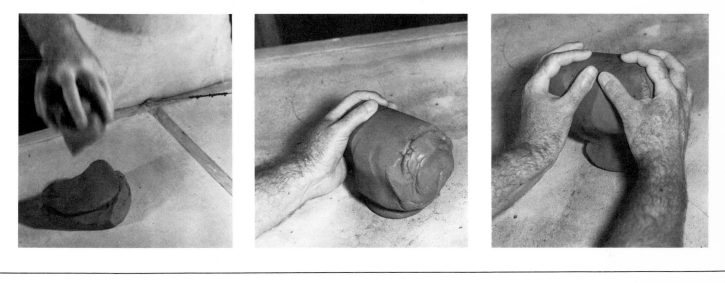

10. Lean into the clay with the arms and body. The heel of the left hand bites into the mass and starts the clay rotating around the point of the cone.

11. The right hand stays in approximately the same position while the left hand reaches behind the form and pulls it up onto the pointed end. The motion in Fig. 10 starts the cycle again.

12. Repeat the wedging perhaps 50–100 times. The form will look like this. As the clay spirals around it is given a thorough kneading; tension on the surface pops open the air bubbles.

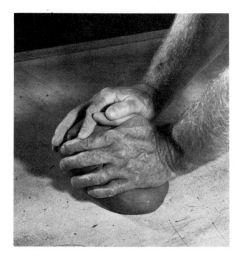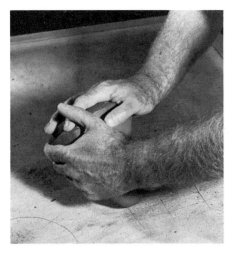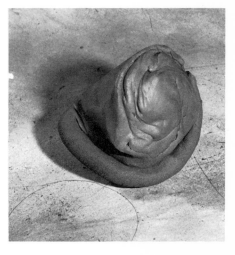

CENTERING

To throw a clay form on the wheel, you must first center a ball of clay on the wheelhead. This might appear easy enough to do, but, as Bernard Leach has said, the clay actually has a preference for any place other than the center. In addition, the clay should be centered in a form that is not difficult to open and lift. A suitable form for beginners is a hemisphere.

Centering can be accomplished by using the correct hand pressures. There must be steady pressure inward (horizontally) to put the clay on a true axis and prevent it

1. Begin with a ball of well-wedged clay that has been patted into a spherical form. An amount that fits comfortably in the hand is easiest to use.

2. Throw the ball with some force as nearly into the center of the wheelhead as you can. The purpose is to stick the clay firmly. The wheel may be at rest or moving very slowly.

3. Paddle the mass rather vigorously to further stick it and move it nearer the center. Enough force is exerted so that the clay is slapped and pushed into a hemispherical form.

7. The cone is forced higher. If the clay is not changing shape, push harder. If the clay begins to sway in a circle, push the mass away from the body while continuing to press inward.

8. Now the clay is pushed down. The left hand pulls the mass into the center to prevent pancaking while the right palm forces the clay downward. Stay relaxed at the waist. Add water frequently.

9. Still pushing downward, the fingers are firm and exert the same pressures. When the hands leave the clay (slowly, not jerked away), the mass should be centered.

from pancaking outward. There must also be pressure downward to push the clay to the desired hemispherical form. While these pressures are being exerted, do not suddenly jerk the hands from the clay or it will at once spin off-center in a most erratic fashion. As long as the need for the two essential pressures is understood and met, the position of the hands may be varied to suit the individual. There is no single, correct way to center. Try to stay relaxed while working. Brace your arms against your body and hunch over the clay. Lubricate the clay surface frequently.

During centering, the wheel should spin quite fast. A right-handed person should turn it counterclockwise. A left-handed person may, if he wishes, turn the wheel clockwise and reverse all the subsequently given hand positions. (Some electric wheels, however, do not reverse direction.)

If the clay ball is thrown onto a plaster bat rather than the metal wheelhead, dampen the plaster first; otherwise the clay may not adhere firmly.

4. Water is used for the first time. Drip some onto the clay with an elephant ear sponge to lubricate the surface. If not enough water is used, the hands will stick to the clay mass.

5. The hands are in position to center. They cup the clay firmly and press inward. The fingers are evenly spaced. The body is relaxed with arms braced at the sides. Bend low over the work.

6. The wheel spins at a fast speed. Pressure inward forces the clay up and into a cone. Let it rise beneath the thumbs. If the force of the hands slows the wheel, increase its speed.

10. Repetition of the above steps may be necessary. To steady the clay, press inward with the fingers, downward with the thumbs, and away from the body with the arms.

11. This alternate position for centering may be helpful. Here, the right elbow is tucked into the stomach as the two hands, thumbs touching, squeeze toward the center.

12. In this position the hands are put to the front and the clay is pulled toward the body. Keep pressing inward at the same time. Try experimenting with personal variations of these hand positions.

OPENING

Beginners on the wheel often have difficulty knowing when the clay is centered. You can tell by watching the form spin: if it is truly centered its profile will remain constant. Or, if a pencil point is held against the edge of the turning clay it will make an even mark when the form is on center. You will soon come to know the feel of a centered form by lightly cupping the hands over the top of the spinning clay. If there is no weaving or swaying back and forth, the form is probably spinning true.

During opening, a hole, whose axis must also be kept

1. When you want to take your hands off the clay, let up the pressure gradually so that the mass does not spin off-center. The ball shown here has a hemispherical form and is ready to be opened.

2. One common method of opening the centered form is shown in this photograph. A wedge of fingers held tightly together drives a hole into the mass of clay.

3. With this second method, the fingers encircle the form and exert little pressure. They merely glide along the wet sides and steady the thumb tips which push downward into the center of the clay.

7. The rim may become thin and start to wobble off-center. Strengthen, compact, and re-align the clay by laying the edge of the fingers across the rim and pressing downward.

8. This illustration and the following cutaway show the opening being widened at the bottom. Interlocked fingertips of both hands slowly pull the clay wall backward toward the body.

9. Keep the arms braced against your sides. As the curved fingers bite into the clay, an undercut is formed. Straightening the fingers will force the wall into a more vertical position.

centered, is driven into the clay. This hole is then widened so that the wall will be properly positioned for lifting. To keep the form on center while the hole is being enlarged, be sure to pull the clay in only one direction—backward, toward the body. Whenever working at the wheel—during centering, opening, lifting, and shaping—cultivate the habit of bracing the arms against your sides. You will be much steadier.

Use the needle frequently to be sure the floor is the correct thickness—1/4 to 3/8 inch is an average one. A

hatpin, dental tool, or a sewing needle stuck into the eraser-end of a pencil make good substitutes if a dissecting needle is not available. The wheel should spin fast although it may go a bit more slowly than it did during centering.

When the mass of clay being thrown is considerably larger than the one shown here, it can be opened more easily with the finger-wedge (fig. 2) than with the thumbs (fig. 3). This may be seen in later photographs, e.g., page 90, fig. 2.

4. The thumbs push deeper. This method is obviously unsuited to opening larger forms that require holes to a depth greater than the length of the thumbs. Use the finger-wedge in such cases.

5. Throughout this book, a dissecting needle is used to trim edges and determine the thickness of the bottom. Here, the needle is pushed into the center of the opening and down to the wheelhead.

6. Running a fingertip down the needle to the floor will determine the clay's thickness. This photograph also shows the V-shaped opening that the thumbs tend to make.

10. Here is something to avoid. Do not open the clay by pulling laterally in opposite directions. The form will almost certainly, and very quickly, spin off-center and out of control.

11. This cutaway shows the opened form. The floor is flat. The interior space is approximately cylindrical. In preparation for lifting, an undercut is left on the inside at the base.

12. The exterior wall is also given an undercut. The right-hand fingertips, held steady by the left hand, bite into the clay at the wheelhead.

 **LIFTING**

After the clay has been opened, the wall must be lifted, or pulled up, or raised; any of these words can serve to describe the action whereby the clay suddenly seems to come alive and assume a rapidly changing form. The aim of lifting, as we shall call it, is twofold: to raise the wall and at the same time to thin it. How high the wall can be lifted depends upon the shape of the opened mass and the amount of clay that was centered. Obviously, the thickness of the wall is also a factor, but it should remain a constant one. One-quarter inch, plus or minus,

1. For the strength and control needed to lift the clay wall, many potters use the knuckle and thumb of the right hand in one of the two positions shown here.

2. The left fingers, kept together and curved slightly, form a plane which is parallel to that of the knuckle and thumb. The left thumb holds the hands together as a lifting unit.

3. The knuckle and the fingertips are directly opposite, on the right-hand side of the form. To lift the clay, they must be squeezed closer together than the thickness of the wall above them.

7. As the top grows thinner, the clay is strengthened by compressing the rim with the edge of the index finger. Using light pressure, the left hand steadies the wall and keeps it from buckling.

8. If the rim flares out because of centrifugal force or too much pressure from the inside hand, collar it in by encircling and constricting the clay with the fingers and thumbs.

9. Several lifts, probably three or four, will be needed to raise the cylinder and give the wall an even thickness from top to bottom. Keep the arms against the body while working.

is a suitable wall thickness for which to strive—at least until you start making quite large forms.

A cylinder was not chosen arbitrarily for these photographs. Lifting normally produces a cylinder; it is the basic form to master. Whether tall or short, all other forms develop from it.

Here are some general things to remember. All of the hand positions shown now and subsequently assume that the wheel is turning counterclockwise. Keep water out of the bottom of the pot. If left there, it will soften the base. Lift it out with a sponge while the wheel is moving. Bend over the clay; get close to it. Keep the hands braced together when possible, and remove them from the spinning clay gradually and gently. If your cylinder does not grow taller, press into the wall more firmly. Common defects include the twisted cylinder—the wall has probably become too thin—and the cylinder with a constantly widening rim—the inside hand is leaning on the top edge and pushing it out.

4. While maintaining the pressure, lift the hands slowly and evenly. Pulling slightly inward will give the cylinder a taper and help to counteract centrifugal force.

5. After each lift, make an undercut on the outside so that the knuckle can once again get beneath the mass. While lifting (and while trimming the lip with a needle), keep the wheel moving rapidly.

6. The inside should be undercut, too. Place the fingertips on the floor and pull backward gently. Hold steady so that the cut stays on center.

10. A needle can be used to trim and level the edge. Hold it like a pencil and brace it against the left thumb. The fingers and thumb of the left hand glide lightly over the clay surface.

11. Without lunging, slowly push the needle into the clay wall until it hits the middle finger of the left hand. After cutting all around the rim, lift off the detached strip.

12. A flat, sharp-edged rim is left after trimming. Using both hands, drape an elephant ear sponge or a piece of chamois over the rim to round and refine it.

SHAPING

Innumerable forms that are essentially cylindrical in nature can be thrown from the cylinder shown in fig. 3; however, you should bear in mind the following: first, a more lively and exciting shape results from paying attention to subtle relationships—of height to width, convexity to concavity, etc.,—and to the character of the lip and foot, the ends of the line, which are always so important. Second, the form shown in fig. 3, a tall cylinder whose walls are approximately even in thickness, is not the proper one to begin with if you want to

1. When lifting keep the right-hand knuckle and thumb flat against the wall and opposite the inside fingertips. Tuck the fingers under a roll of clay and move it upward. Hunch over the work.

2. To steady a wobbly cylinder, overcome the effects of centrifugal force, or begin a tapering action, grip the clay in a stranglehold and squeeze in gently. This is called collaring.

3. A basic maneuver—introducing a convexity to a vertical wall—is begun. Pressure from the inside fingers forces the clay outward. The hands continue to rise as the curve develops.

7. The main curve is terminated more abruptly as the fingertips bite in and leave a band at the lip. Near the top the hands may be braced; earlier they have had to work independently.

8. Collaring—perhaps the quickest and most reliable method of constricting a large expanse of clay—is employed again. Touch the thumbs together and encircle as much of the form as possible.

9. The lower section of the pot is refined and pushed in to its final shape. It may be helpful occasionally to close your eyes, imagine a curve, and try to "feel" it into being.

make a wide, flaring bowl, or a globe, or some other non-cylindrical form. To achieve such shapes, adjustments during centering, opening, and lifting are necessary and will be discussed in later chapters.

During shaping, the wheel goes fast, slowing down at moments when finer control is needed. When the wheel slows, lift the hands more slowly; there must always be a correlation between the two. Try to throw using as little water as possible. Not much finger pressure inward or outward is needed to constrict or distend the form

significantly. Notice that after the cylinder has been pulled up, the knuckle is no longer used on the outside. While shaping, greater sensitivity to the changing profile can be achieved with the fingertips. Try holding the fingertips in different ways to discover or "invent" a lip that will harmonize with the rest of the form.

4. Stop working at any time (always removing the hands gradually) if the surface of the clay becomes too dry. With the throwing sponge trickle water down the spinning walls.

5. The inside fingers are bunched together and slightly arched. As they move upward, they push the clay wall out into a gentle arc. The outside fingers help to stabilize and support the curve.

6. The outside fingers, which a moment ago were passive and supportive, now assume an active role. Inward pressure from the right hand forces the clay into a concave form.

10. The band at the rim (which could have been left as an attractive, concluding form) is now removed. The wall is pushed outward as pressure downward on the lip compresses and thickens the clay.

11. If enough clay has been left at the lip (fig. 10), it can be widened considerably. A full flare is given to the rim by folding the clay over the supporting, outside fingers.

12. After completion, many forms can be trimmed in a simple, rapid manner while still on the wheel. Here excess clay is being cut away with the bevelled edge of a tongue depressor.

REMOVING THE FORM

Many stable, cylindrical forms can be lifted from the wheelhead with the palms of the hands immediately after throwing, particularly if only a small amount of water has been used. But, at best, picking up a wet pot in this way is chancy. On the other hand, the method illustrated here is nearly foolproof and enables one to remove not only cylindrical forms but more complex ones as well. If a form goes out-of-round during removal, it can be brought back when the pot is inverted at the leather-hard stage.

1. To make a cutoff wire, twist two strands of thin wire together and attach the ends to metal washers. Keep the wire taut and pressed onto the wheelhead as it is pulled beneath the pot.

2. Wet one-half of the wheelhead with water or thin slip. A floor tile covered with a wet paper towel is then braced against the body and placed slightly lower than the edge of the wheelhead.

3. Using all the fingers to distribute the pressure against the clay, reach around the pot, grasp it lightly at the base, and tilt it gently toward the tile.

4. Here is a frontal view of the pot being tilted. It is essential that the hands be dry. If moist, they will slide on the wet clay and not get a firm grasp on it.

5. The pot is now pulled backward. As soon as it touches the water and separates from the clay on the wheelhead, it can be moved onto the tile quickly and easily.

6. When the pot has become leather-hard, the bottom edge will need some final attention. It can be smoothed with a finger or given a more extensive, finished trim as was done on page 30, fig. 2.

DRYING THE FORM

If possible, dry a piece upside down or lying on its side. Try to dry pieces evenly—whether slowly or quickly. A pot that is completely dry in one place and still wet in another may eventually crack. Avoid wheel-forms with thin tops and heavy bottoms; such pieces will dry unevenly. Keep drying pots away from strong drafts and extremes of temperature, e.g., an open window or a firing kiln. For pots to survive the drying stage, thoughtful and time-consuming attention must often be given to them.

1. Lightly rub your fingers along the rim. When you no longer pick up clay, the pot is leather-hard—that is, the clay is rigid, leathery, and about half dry. Invert the pot on a flat surface.

2. If you have waited too long and the top is considerably drier than the bottom, wrap a piece of light plastic cloth around the rim to retard further drying for a while.

3. If the top is unusually fragile or has complex, projecting forms which make it impractical to invert the pot, drape a plastic cloth over the upper area to prevent rapid drying.

4. If a flat surface is not available, or a form is too tall, unstable, or cannot be inverted for reasons already mentioned, dowels or flat sticks will help to promote even drying.

5. Parts which are thin and exposed to the air on all sides will dry first and may crack unless special attention is given to them.

6. Wrapping a handle or a thin, projecting form with plastic or a moistened paper towel can save the day—and the pot. Clays vary. some are quite strong while drying; others crack readily.

19

USING A BAT

A bat is a plaster disc that can be attached to the wheelhead by mechanical means or with a layer of clay slip. There are several advantages to using a bat: you can throw a form whose base is wider than the wheelhead; and you can remove a piece—perhaps a large bowl or an unusually thin or precarious form which ordinarily would be difficult to lift off without distortion or collapse—so that the wheel may immediately be used again. A pot can be cut from the bat with a twisted wire in the usual manner.

1. Soak plastic clay or clay scraps in water until clay slip, which has a thick, creamy consistency, has formed. The bat should be dry, or nearly so, and scraped reasonably free of dried clay.

2. Rub a liberal coating of clay slip onto the plaster bat and the wheelhead. Heavy lumps should be avoided. If the clay film is too thin, the bat will not adhere properly.

3. Vigorously slide the two surfaces together. There is perhaps a half minute to center the bat before the clay sandwich hardens, after which time the bat can no longer be moved.

4. For throwing, it is not necessary that the bat be perfectly centered on the wheelhead. Touch a pencil to the spinning bat and a centered circle will be marked on the plaster.

5. Moisten the bat with thin slip or water before beginning to throw. With some force and as much accuracy as possible, throw the clay ball into the marked circle.

6. Gently insert a fettling knife between the plaster and the wheelhead to remove the bat. Be careful. If the seal breaks abruptly and the bat bounces, the wet pot on the bat may collapse.

2/BOWLS AND TRIMMING

BOWL I

When making a more open form—a bowl with a rounded bottom whose width exceeds its height for example—there must be some modifications in the method given for throwing a cylinder. Rather than being hemispherical, the clay is centered in a wide, flat shape which prefigures and influences the final form. The floor, instead of being flat, is curved during opening, and the curve is continued and developed in the wall. For a seamless transition between floor and wall, one must be careful while opening not to make deep

1. To center a wide, low form, try a different hand position. The left hand holds steady, with some pressure to the center, while the right hand presses downward and levels the top.

2. Instead of opening the clay by pulling straight across the bottom, begin a curving floor by grdually lifting the fingers as they move to the outside edge.

3. This cutaway shows the developing curve of the floor which is lower in the center than at the edges. During opening, use the dissecting needle at various points to check the thickness of the bottom.

7. The bowl is drawn out again. Start from the base and make an even, rhythmic lift. There should be a smooth transition between the curve of the floor and the curve of the wall.

8. Unless the body is bent to one side to watch the curve develop, an interesting and well-proportioned form may be missed. The shape of the inside space is important, too.

9. A complex or simple form can be given to the lip. Perhaps the simplest and easiest lip is made by lightly folding an elephant ear sponge over the rim.

undercuts on the inside. As they are lifted outward, the walls must remain thick enough so that the clay can be eased into the desired curve. If the clay is given its normal thickness too quickly, the walls may be stretched much too thin when the curve is finally added.

As the diameter widens, the lip thins and the clay weakens. Compacting the lip frequently will give the clay extra strength and prevent splitting. Watch the outside, the profile of the form, but also be aware of the way the space is being designed on the inside of the bowl. Close your eyes at some point and try to "feel" the curve into existence.

The speed of the wheel is all-important; it may vary from moving quite rapidly, as during centering and opening, to going quite slowly when the lip reaches its final diameter. Too abrupt a stop or change in speed can throw the bowl off-center or collapse it in an instant.

4. The same lifting position is used when making a bowl—the knuckle and fingertips are opposite, the hands are joined. But instead of being lifted vertically, the clay wall is aimed outward.

5. The wall is curved by pushing the inside fingers outward as the hands rise. Bunching the fingertips of the right hand to substitute for the knuckle affords a greater degree of control.

6. As the rim widens, the clay gets stretched thinner. To strengthen and thicken the rim, press downward with the edge of a finger while steadying the wall with the left hand.

10. If the transition between floor and wall is not smooth enough, the curved edge of a metal rib can help. Tilt the rib toward the body to avoid gouging deeply into the clay.

11. As it cuts, the rib will leave a smooth surface. This may remain or finger rings can be run in again, as shown here, with the aid of a sponge.

12. The bat is freed from the wheelhead by sliding a fettling knife between the two. Care must be taken to release the bat gently. Otherwise, the wet, fragile bowl may jiggle and deform.

PREPARING FOR TRIMMING

A bowl may be cut from the bat with a twisted wire or will naturally separate from the bat when the plaster has partially dried the bottom. The latter method was utilized here. Once the bottom thickness has been determined, the bowl is inverted. But before turning it over, study the inner space and try to retain an image of the curvature near the bottom. If the diameter of the bowl is the same as or larger than that of the wheelhead, it should be trimmed on a plaster bat or a circle of plywood cut with a sabre saw. The weight of such a bowl

1. A needle or pencil, held vertically, touches the center of the bottom of the form. Push the index finger down the side until it lines up with the outside edges of the form.

2. If you do not want to bend over far enough to see when that point is reached, you can use a thin strip of wood or a metal ruler across the top.

3. Here is a frontal view of fig. 2. The tip of the index finger is touching the needle at the point where it meets the bottom edge of the wooden strip.

7. Spin the wheel and slowly move a pencil tip until it touches the side near the area to be trimmed. If a line is inscribed all the way around, the bowl is centered.

8. If the line does not encircle the surface, the bowl will need to be centered. Locate the length of the line, which is shown here between the index fingers.

9. Bisect the line with a small mark. That mark should be pushed or pulled directly toward the center of the wheel—in the direction of the paper arrow.

will probably be sufficient to hold the plaster bat or plywood in place so that neither will need to be attached to the wheelhead with slip.

Center the bowl's base. It is useless to have the rim centered if the base is nowhere near alignment. You may have to compromise and accept something less than a perfect centering, particularly if the bowl was not thrown true.

A much quicker method of centering, though one more difficult to learn (and to photograph), is not pictured. Well worth the effort, when finally mastered, it makes centering the inverted piece a simple and rapid process. When the spinning, uncentered form comes closest to the spot where you are holding your open hand—at the right side of the wheelhead—gently tap the bowl toward the center of the wheelhead. When it makes another revolution, tap it again, and so on, until the form is aligned. You must develop the necessary rhythm to tap the bowl inward three or four times at exactly the right instant.

4. Now place the needle against the outside edge of the pot. The distance between the tip of the finger and the top of the bowl is equal to the thickness of the bottom.

5. Study the bowl carefully from different angles and consider what diameter you want the foot to be. Laying a strip of paper on the inside (and outside) may be helpful.

6. After being inverted, the bowl must be centered. Using the concentric wheelhead rings can help, particularly if the piece was thrown on center. Another method is shown in the next photographs.

10. In a second test the pencil marked a much longer line, this time shown between the middle fingers. The bowl needs pushing again, gently, still in the direction of the paper arrow.

11. When finally centered, the bowl must be attached to the wheelhead. While holding it steady, lay three or four coils around the base. Press the clay downward to force it against the bowl.

12. Do not push the clay too roughly against the side; it may crack the lip. The strip of paper utilized in fig. 5 has been laid on the top to establish a tentative diameter.

TRIMMING THE BOWL

There is no one "correct" diameter to make the foot of a given bowl. Rather, you must try to visualize a width that you think will give the bowl stable support and a pleasing relationship with its bulk and curvature.

It is not uncommon for a beginner to cut through the side of a bowl while trimming it, although more often than not the clay will start to give when that moment is nearly at hand. Some potters try to get a sense of the thickness of the wall by tapping it with a finger. While this method is not a precise one, some practice will

1. A sharp-edged, right-angled trimming tool has been chosen to cut the bowl. After the first cut, the diameter of the foot can be decreased but it cannot easily be made larger.

2. A memory of the inside space must now begin to guide the trimming. Hold the tool firmly, but be prepared to loosen your grip if the tool suddenly catches and bites too deeply in the clay.

3. In figs. 2 and 3 excess clay is being shaved away. If the pot has been brought to the proper degree of dryness, the shavings will come off in long curls.

7. The inside diameter of the foot-ring is being located and cut. The width of the ring may vary according to the size of the bowl, the kind of clay being used, the style of the potter, etc.

8. The interior clay is cut away. The trimming tool begins in the center and moves out toward the foot-ring's inner edge. Care must be taken to avoid cutting into the ring itself.

9. The clay inside the foot-ring was not trimmed flat, but, rather, was given a shallow arc to follow the slight curve inside the bowl. The inside edge is being bevelled to eliminate sharpness.

enable you to distinguish between a thick wall and a thin one. If you have doubts, pick up the bowl and feel its thickness, or use a pair of pottery calipers to determine if you have cut to the correct depth. When the bowl has been properly trimmed, the wall should be of uniform thickness—down one side, across the bottom, and up the other side. Avoid cutting too high on the bowl; otherwise the form will begin to lose its plastic character and assume a wooden, mechanical appearance.

Trimming may be done with any device that will remove excess clay. Potters use knives, ribs, and tools made specifically for the purpose. Get several rigid, wire-loop or steel-band tools which provide a variety of cutting arcs and angles.

4. More clay is shaved off. The left hand supports and steadies the right hand. If the clay is too wet to trim, it will stick to the tool. If too dry, it will come off in powder and dull the tool.

5. The curve of the inside is being followed. Move the tool slowly up and down, never backward and forward. Here, the bowl is being shaved below the foot to create a more gradual modulation.

6. The relationship of the foot (now being formed) to the bowl may be one of sharp contrast or almost imperceptible transition. It can be cut to curve, slant inward or outward, or stand vertically.

10. Trimmed edges left sharp can chip easily before a pot is fired and when it is used after firing. Conclude the trimming by bevelling or rounding both inner and outer edges of the foot-ring.

11. A straight edge can help you avoid cutting through the bottom. The center of the bottom, about 3/8 inch thick before trimming, was cut to a depth of 1/8 inch, leaving the clay a normal 1/4 inch thickness.

12. Allow the air to dry the bottom and sides of an open form evenly and safely by placing it upside-down on a flat surface. The rim will dry level as well.

BOWLS II, III

To throw forms similar to those shown here, only slight adjustments need be made in the techniques described earlier. In the first bowl the fingers do not rise and curve the bottom during opening but move flat across the floor as was done in the cylinder. The fingers should press down hard in their movement across the bottom. Such pressure will compact and strengthen the clay and render it less likely to crack while drying—a common hazard in wide, flat-bottomed bowls.

The second bowl was begun from a hemispherical

1. The clay is being opened from a low, wide form, and the wall is being pulled back to a vertical position. Hands interlock and fingertips press down to strengthen the clay floor.

2. Several lifts thin the wall as greater pressure from the inside hand pushes the clay outward. To prevent splitting and cracking as it widens, the lip is kept thick.

3. With the fingers of the right hand giving support from underneath, the clay is flared and gently folded over. A change of direction at the lip will help to prevent warpage during firing.

7. No attempt is made to give the clay a final form until the wall is near its normal thickness. Lifting continues, outward. Brace the hands together when possible for steadiness.

8. Clay at the lip is pressed together and thickened. Laying the index finger flat on the edge accomplishes this while other fingers support the wall and keep it from twisting.

9. Shaping has begun and the body is bent to one side to watch the form develop. Clay is pushed from the inside against the fingertips; both hands rise together in a rhythmic arc.

28

ball of clay much like the one centered and thrown into a cylinder, but, whereas the cylinder wall was pulled up vertically, or even given a slight taper inward, the bowl wall is aimed outward from the first lift. It is possible to make a bowl with an even smaller base than the one shown here, in which case, very little, if any, opening of the clay is necessary. After a hole has been pushed into the centered mass in the usual V shape, immediately make a deep undercut with the knuckle and start pulling the wall up and outward. The bowl will at once assume a conical form as the inside space converges to an almost pointed bottom. To reach a full-flared diameter, however, the clay must be kept thick and the lip frequently compacted.

4. The bowl may be cut from the bat with a wire or left to break free when the plaster starts to dry the bottom. Preliminary trimming is being done with the sharply cut edge of a tongue depressor.

5. To make a tall bowl with a small foot, the clay is centered and opened from a narrow base. Here, as lifting begins, the knuckle undercuts the base and starts the clay moving upward.

6. Beginning at the wheelhead, the hands move outward as they rise. A heavy roll of clay is kept at the top edge to provide for the eventual wide flare of the lip.

10. Take several gradual lifts to bring the bowl to its final flare. Instead of using the elephant ear sponge to finish the lip, try holding the fingers in different positions to form the edge.

11. With hands touching for stability, the clay wall is draped over the outside fingers. A sturdy lip makes a strong visual conclusion and inhibits deformation during firing.

12. Since very little water was used during throwing and the form is a relatively stable one, the bowl was cut free with a twisted wire and immediately lifted off the wheel.

29

TRIMMING THE BOWLS

Remember that the clay lugs which hold a pot to the wheelhead may crack the lip if they are pushed too vigorously against it. The decision not to have a high foot on the flat-bottomed bowl was made before the pot was thrown. Accordingly, the floor was kept to a near-normal thickness. In such cases, it is optional whether to trim clay from the center of the bottom. If the bowl is kept as it was cut from the bat or the wheelhead, the bottom will retain the attractive whorl left by the twisted wire.

1. The contrasting and elevating form of a high foot is not needed on a flat-bottomed bowl whose walls do not have a pronounced curve or flare.

2. Less than 1/8 inch of clay was trimmed from the center, leaving a low, rounded footing at the edge. Sometimes a wide bottom will warp and bulge outward. The indentation should minimize that.

3. An open form with a flat floor is somewhat more prone to crack during drying. Turn the bowl upside down on its rim and cover the walls with plastic if they begin to dry more quickly than the bottom.

4. The inside curve of the form is followed during trimming. A rough surface left from the cutting tool may be smoothed with a wooden rib or stick held against the spinning pot (page 58, fig. 4).

5. After the height and angle of the foot have been defined, establish the inner diameter of the ring with a vertical cut. Trim from the center toward the cut. Bevel or round the edges.

6. A tall bowl with a sweeping flare and a narrow base may be enhanced by a high foot. This one affords a contrast and lifts the bowl for display with a measure of elegance.

ball of clay much like the one centered and thrown into a cylinder, but, whereas the cylinder wall was pulled up vertically, or even given a slight taper inward, the bowl wall is aimed outward from the first lift. It is possible to make a bowl with an even smaller base than the one shown here, in which case, very little, if any, opening of the clay is necessary. After a hole has been pushed into the centered mass in the usual V shape, immediately make a deep undercut with the knuckle and start pulling the wall up and outward. The bowl will at once assume a conical form as the inside space converges to an almost pointed bottom. To reach a full-flared diameter, however, the clay must be kept thick and the lip frequently compacted.

4. The bowl may be cut from the bat with a wire or left to break free when the plaster starts to dry the bottom. Preliminary trimming is being done with the sharply cut edge of a tongue depressor.

5. To make a tall bowl with a small foot, the clay is centered and opened from a narrow base. Here, as lifting begins, the knuckle undercuts the base and starts the clay moving upward.

6. Beginning at the wheelhead, the hands move outward as they rise. A heavy roll of clay is kept at the top edge to provide for the eventual wide flare of the lip.

10. Take several gradual lifts to bring the bowl to its final flare. Instead of using the elephant ear sponge to finish the lip, try holding the fingers in different positions to form the edge.

11. With hands touching for stability, the clay wall is draped over the outside fingers. A sturdy lip makes a strong visual conclusion and inhibits deformation during firing.

12. Since very little water was used during throwing and the form is a relatively stable one, the bowl was cut free with a twisted wire and immediately lifted off the wheel.

TRIMMING THE BOWLS

Remember that the clay lugs which hold a pot to the wheelhead may crack the lip if they are pushed too vigorously against it. The decision not to have a high foot on the flat-bottomed bowl was made before the pot was thrown. Accordingly, the floor was kept to a near-normal thickness. In such cases, it is optional whether to trim clay from the center of the bottom. If the bowl is kept as it was cut from the bat or the wheelhead, the bottom will retain the attractive whorl left by the twisted wire.

1. The contrasting and elevating form of a high foot is not needed on a flat-bottomed bowl whose walls do not have a pronounced curve or flare.

2. Less than 1/8 inch of clay was trimmed from the center, leaving a low, rounded foot-ring at the edge. Sometimes a wide bottom will warp and bulge outward. The indentation should minimize that.

3. An open form with a flat floor is somewhat more prone to crack during drying. Turn the bowl upside down on its rim and cover the walls with plastic if they begin to dry more quickly than the bottom.

4. The inside curve of the form is followed during trimming. A rough surface left from the cutting tool may be smoothed with a wooden rib or stick held against the spinning pot (page 58, fig. 4).

5. After the height and angle of the foot have been defined, establish the inner diameter of the ring with a vertical cut. Trim rrom the center toward the cut. Bevel or round the edges.

6. A tall bowl with a sweeping flare and a narrow base may be enhanced by a high foot. This one affords a contrast and lifts the bowl for display with a measure of elegance.

3/PITCHERS, HANDLES, AND PLATES

PITCHER

A well-made pitcher should be attractive to look at and pleasurable to use. The same might be said of any pot, but it bears mentioning here because the body of the pitcher is part of an ensemble. You may make beautiful components—handles and bodies—but if they do not belong together—if the handle is too large, too small, or improperly placed on the side of the body—the pitcher will not be attractive. It is essential, therefore, to give some thought to (and have some feeling about) not only the parts themselves but how they look together.

1. The pitcher made here is a tall variant of a cylinder. Accordingly, the clay is centered in a hemispherical form. Pressure from both hands toward the middle completes the centering.

2. After each lift, an undercut is made to enable the knuckle and fingers to grab hold of the clay more easily. The inward taper helps to keep the form under control.

3. As the wheel spins, centrifugal force constantly widens the top. Collaring brings the top in and in so doing thickens the rim.

7. Shaping continues. The lip has been folded over in a flare and given its final shape with a sponge. The belly of the pot is being pushed out to a more substantial form.

8. Water should not be left inside the pot. In narrow spaces a sponge works well when held to a dowel with a rubber band. Always spin the wheel while removing the water.

9. A spout is formed as the clay is gently and repeatedly teased outward with a wet finger. To steady the form, the left thumb and index finger push inward in opposition.

Although certain aspects of the pitcher's functionality are discussed in the following pages, here are some thoughts relative to the body of the form. The pitcher should be of normal thickness or perhaps even a bit on the thin side. If too heavy, it will be unpleasant to hold and pour from when filled with liquid. Trim the bottom properly; excessive weight there is annoying for the same reason. Think about the amount of space (and its shape) needed to put your fingers between the handle and side of the pitcher. Finally, make a spout immedi-

ately after the pitcher body has been thrown. A spout should have an attractive curve and an edge that will draw the last drops back into the pitcher rather than allow them to flow down the outside.

4. Shaping has begun. The belly has been given a first curve and bunched fingertips now press inward at the wheelhead to narrow the diameter of the base.

5. A second collaring constricts the cylinder again. While the thumbs and fingers encircle the clay, the hands move upward and help to define the form of the piece.

6. If the lip seems uneven, use a needle to cut off a small strip. Practice until as little as 1/8 inch can be satisfactorily trimmed. When the clay is mushy, stop the wheel to remove the trimmed strip.

10. An optional treatment consists of forming a channel for the flowing liquid. A quick movement downward on both sides by the fingertips creates these channel grooves.

11. Time can often be saved by trimming wet pots rather than leather-hard ones. Here, excess clay is being shaved away with the angled edge of a wooden rib.

12. This close-up view of the lip shows the clay eased out to a sharp edge—a form that will stop a liquid from running down the outer wall of the pitcher and draw it back inside.

PULLING A HANDLE I

A simple handle can be made by rolling a coil of clay, bending it into a loop, and attaching it to the pitcher body when both are near the leather-hard stage. Cutting a strip from a slab flattened with a rolling pin will also give a serviceable handle that is quick and easy to form.

A third kind of handle, considerably more difficult to make, is the one which potters have traditionally used. Called a pulled handle, it is particularly complementary to a wheel-thrown form, whereas the coil and slab handles may seem incompatible with it. The harmony

1. Push a well-wedged piece of clay that is neither mushy or unusually hard into a conical form. Grasp it firmly, in either hand, with the pointed end downward.

2. While the handle is being formed, the pulling hand must be kept wet, so work near a running faucet or a basin of water. Start to apply pressure to the clay, slowly pulling downward.

3. A tongue will begin to develop. Keep wetting the hand. Do not jerk, stretch, or pinch the clay. Keep the surface moist and slippery. Pull rhythmically, scarcely feeling the clay's resistance.

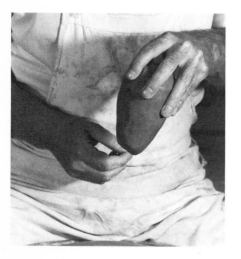

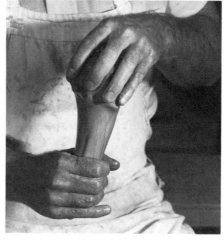

7. At this stage not much pressure is needed, but keep the surfaces slippery. If the fingers are too dry or they jerk too vigorously, the clay may crack or pull apart.

8. Now that the handle has reached a suitable length and form, the end of the tongue is picked up and given the desired loop. Do not jiggle or be jostled at this moment.

9. The curve of the handle can be adjusted according to where the tongue is pushed against the clay ball. If too much water was used, the loop will collapse.

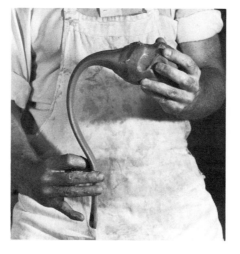

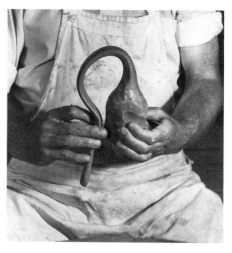

between a wheel-pot and a pulled handle exists because both of them are sophisticated, machined forms which identify clay as a plastic material, highly responsive to the touch of the hand.

However, unless the clay has been perfectly wedged, it will not be possible to pull the handle satisfactorily. Lumps, splits, and other irregularities will spoil its sleek, fluid taper. Even after proper wedging, some clays, particularly if they have been newly prepared, will crack when the loop is formed. To avoid this, use more water during the pulling. If that does not work, wedge a thimbleful of vinegar into a lump of clay and store it in a plastic bag for a few days. Its plasticity should be noticeably improved.

4. Do not rotate or twist the clay while it is being pulled. As the tongue lengthens, lessen somewhat the teasing/pulling pressure of the hand. Wet the hand before each pull.

5. To pull a handle of a particular cross section—round, flat, oval, etc.—and keep the section constant, it is necessary to hold the finger position steady during the length of the pull.

6. If the tongue gets too long, pinch off the end. Keep pulling until the section and length appear right. Here the handle is being shaped between the index and middle fingers for a flatter cross section.

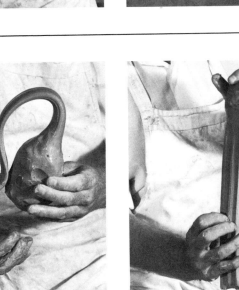

10. If too little water was used, the clay may crack. Here the tongue has been attached lightly to the side of the cone and the excess clay pinched off.

11. Another handle is being pulled. A different cross section can be formed by using the fingertips or the thumb to pull grooves into the clay. As before, pull rhythmically, from top to bottom.

12. After a handle has been looped to the desired curve, it should be set aside on the cone to harden a bit before being cut and attached to the pitcher.

ATTACHING THE HANDLE

Somewhat like a photographer who makes numerous exposures hoping to find the perfect image, a potter makes several handles hoping that one of them will be a perfect match for his pitcher. When considering the placement of the handle, apart from its aesthetic character you should keep in mind its utility. It should be positioned so that, when the full pitcher is lifted and poured, the weight will be evenly balanced. If a handle is too near the top, particularly on a tall form, it is difficult to gain the leverage needed to move the pitcher's

1. Finding a good visual relationship between pitcher and handle may prove easier when there is a group of different handles to choose from. These are being allowed to stiffen.

2. Holding the cone and its handle behind the pitcher's profile will give you some indication of where to make the cut. If in doubt, cut to leave extra clay on the handle.

3. Try holding all of the handles against the pitcher in different positions. If the lower wall is thick, trim it before the attachment is made, particularly when the handle is placed this low.

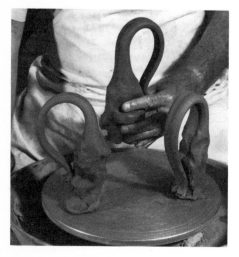

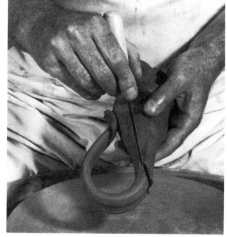

7. With a knife tip, piece of comb, or some other sharp tool, score the areas where the handle will be attached to the pitcher.

8. Both ends of the handle were also roughened. All four surfaces are now being painted with slip, a thick, creamy mixture of clay and water which will act as a glue.

9. The upper end of the handle is pushed firmly against the side of the pitcher which is still soft enough to need a supporting hand on the inside.

weight. Two hands may be necessary to hold and pour it. If a handle is placed too low, it is not easy to pour the pitcher with accuracy, and liquids will tend to slosh out indecorously.

Depending on how the handle was pulled, looped, and attached to the body of the pitcher, it will look more or less as though it grows out of the form. Although an organic relationship between the two is certainly desirable, many potters believe that the method illustrated here is not the best way to achieve it; that in spite of one's best efforts, a preformed handle will always have an alien, stuck-on appearance. Pulling the handle directly on the pitcher is the method favored by many. This technique is discussed in the next section.

4. The space between the handle and the body of the pitcher should be considered carefully—as a visual design factor and as a place to insert the fingers.

5. A fettling knife has been used to cut a concavity that matches the curvature of the pitcher. The small end may be left as it breaks away from the cone of clay.

6. Test the fit of the handle against the curved surface. Be sure that the handle is vertical and placed directly behind the spout. Mark the handle's outline on the side of the pitcher.

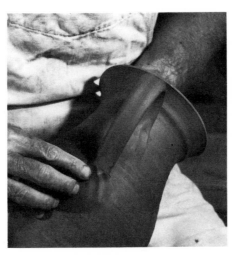

10. After the handle has been checked again for verticality, the lower end is attached. Wiggle it against the pitcher wall to secure the joint.

11. The handle ends can be finished off in several ways. They can be blended smoothly into the side of the pitcher or given a decorative treatment with the fingertip.

12. A handle with a wide, sweeping curve may need to be propped up with a stiff ball of clay as it dries. Loosely wrapping the handle in plastic cloth will retard its drying rate.

PULLING A HANDLE II

If the handle is pulled too strenuously and thin spots develop, remove it and prepare another one. If the side of the pitcher has become too soft, wait awhile before starting again. Each of the two forming methods has its advantages. A handle shaped on the pot has directness, vigor, spontaneity, and an organic character that is highly appealing. On the other hand, preforming does not necessarily exclude those characteristics, and it allows a greater range of handle shapes and a flexibility of approach that is often desirable.

1. Determine where the handle is to be placed. Making some thumbnail sketches may help. Score and lightly slip the area that will receive the thick, butt end of the handle.

2. Start the handle from a cone, keeping it somewhat drier than before. Cut or pinch off the needed section. Since it will be pulled on the pot, the clay tongue should be rather thick.

3. Ram the thick end of the tongue against the slipped surface. Then, using the thumb, work the clay well into the pitcher all the way around the handle.

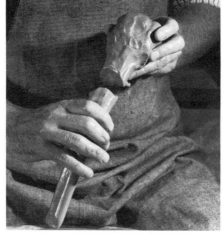

4. During the final pulling, the pitcher may be held in profile. With the top of the form tilted downward, the handle will leave the pitcher at a good angle.

5. A more common method of pulling is to hold the pitcher so that you face the opening. To establish a pleasing taper, pull rhythmically downward from the top of the handle to the bottom.

6. Snip off any excess clay if the tongue grows too long. Gently right the pitcher, form the loop, and attach the bottom of the handle to the side of the form.

DIPPER

Some dippers have two spouts. This enables them to be used by both right- and left-handed persons. However, there is a disadvantage: the handle should then be placed exactly between the spouts; whereas, with a single spout, as shown here, the handle can be moved off-center to accommodate the scooping and pouring motion of a particular individual. Making a dipper requires developing a design and a method of support that will allow the handle to escape serious deformation during firing.

1. A long, tapering handle was cut near the cone to keep a thick end. Placed on its side in a slight curve, it was allowed to dry for about an hour.

2. The end of the handle can be concluded in various ways—pinched with the fingers, left as cut from the cone, or, as here, tapped into a different form with a mallet.

3. The clay is in a soft/firm state, just short of being leather-hard. It retains its curve, yet is plastic enough to be shaped and grooved by the edge of the mallet.

4. Thrown like a small bowl, its spout formed like that of a pitcher, the dipper has been trimmed round on the bottom and dried to the consistency of the handle.

5. Before attaching the handle, move it against the side of the dipper bowl to find a good visual relationship and also one that will permit easy scooping and pouring.

6. Joined to the bowl with slip and solidly welded into place, the handle is supported at several points while it dries. Dry the dipper beneath a loosely draped cover of plastic cloth.

PLATE

Pounding a lump of clay into a symmetrical pancake before centering begins will save time and energy. When the wall is vertical, before shaping is begun (fig. 3), level the lip with a finger or cut it so with the needle. If done at this time, it should not be necessary to trim the lip later when the wall is flared and unstable.

There is a brief logic to certain aspects of plate-making which is not difficult to understand and apply. First, decide the width of the plate you wish to make. I am speaking of plastic width. If you want to consider

1. For maximum use of the plaster surface, center the bat as accurately as possible. Strong pressure downward with the edge of the hand levels the clay mass.

2. With interlocked fingers the clay is being opened. While pulling across the floor, let the fingers rise slightly to develop a shallow curve. Control the bottom thickness by using a needle.

3. While the inside fingers lightly give support to the vertical wall, pressure is applied onto the lip. This will level, stabilize, and strengthen the edge before the plate is shaped.

7. Always determine the outer diameter of the foot-ring first. The wall may settle or fall down during firing if the overhang is too great or the curve too shallow.

8. A cut to the proper depth has been completed and excess clay on the outside is being trimmed away. Trim with care to let the curve continue to the edge of the foot.

9. The inner diameter of the ring is now established with a second vertical cut. A suitable foot-ring thickness for a plate this size is 1/4 to 3/8 inch.

fired width, you must know the firing shrinkage of the clay you are using. Next, center the clay in a low form, at a diameter approximately three to four inches less than that of the desired plate. When the mass has been opened and the wall brought to a vertical position, you should then have enough clay to flare the wall out to a one-and-one-half to two-inch overhang. The wheel must be under complete control at this point and moving quite slowly. The wall should be lowered gradually and supported by the outside hand. If the clay is too thin, or too wet, or the curve too flat, the plate may be lost. Finally, when the plate has been inverted for trimming, consider using a diameter for the foot that is close to the diameter of the centered mass. Such a foot will give good support and be in pleasing proportion to the plate itself.

4. The clay is slowly guided into a curve. Here the outside fingers help to support the wall as it flares away from the base. Work for a smooth transition between floor and wall.

5. To refine the curve or smooth the surface, a flexible metal rib may be used. It can easily gouge the form ruinously unless held firmly and at an acute angle to the clay.

6. If a rib is used on the curve beyond the base, the wall must be supported to prevent its collapse. Throwing rings may be run into the clay again with the fingertips working outward from the center.

10. Starting at the center and trimming out to meet the inner cut removes unwanted clay from inside the foot-ring. Bracing the trimming hand helps to prevent accidental digs and slices.

11. Chipped foot-ring edges can be avoided before and after firing if the ring is bevelled or rounded during trimming. Trim the center deep enough so that the plate does not rock.

12. Conceive of the trimming so that if the foot-ring could be lifted off, the contour of the form would flow unbroken from one edge across the bottom to the opposite side.

41

CUP AND SAUCER

There is no reason why one form must be made before the other. If the saucer is thrown first, it can be kept leather-hard and the cup-well trimmed out once the size of the cup's foot is known. But as soon as one form has been made, take a critical look at it. Its size, shape, thickness, and flamboyancy or simplicity should be considered before making the other form. Remember that a layer of glaze will reduce the size of the cup-well. A cup that fits exactly before firing may not fit at all afterward.

1. So that the piece will not be heavy and cumbersome, be especially careful when trimming—and throwing—a form designed to hold liquid. Here, pottery calipers measure the diameter of the foot-ring.

2. Several small handles were pulled and allowed to stiffen. One whose curve seems suited to the cup will now be attached. The handle could have been thrown directly on the cup instead.

3. The saucer is a small plate and was centered, thrown, and trimmed like one. For support the foot-ring has been placed beneath the cup-well.

4. With a needle or a pencil point mark a few circles on the clay until you find one—using the calipers again—that is a little larger in diameter than the cup's foot-ring.

5. The cup-well has been cut out to a depth of 1/8 inch, plus or minus—an amount that was taken into account when the inside of the foot was trimmed—to avoid a thin bottom.

6. If you are expecting the cup and saucer to be a specific size when completed, you must take into consideration the total shrinkage of your clay, from the plastic to the fired state.

4/LIDS AND JARS

CURVED INSET LID

To be successful, a lid must visually complement its container and fit snugly. Thoughtful consideration and good craftsmanship—in measuring and in throwing and trimming both forms—are required to attain these objectives.

When the double-thick lip is divided, strong pressure is applied downward on the wall. A pot that is globular, too thin, or too wet may give way under this pressure. Allow such pieces to sit for a while (the rim can be covered with light plastic) before splitting the edge. Beating

1. If the rim can be kept level during lifting, it is usually unnecessary to trim it later with a needle. This hand position both levels and strengthens the clay by compacting it.

2. The upper two-thirds of the cylinder is gradually pushed outward against the right fingertips. A double thickness of clay will be left at the top to form a ledge.

3. A double thickness is necessary so that the clay can be divided into a lip and a ledge. The index fingertip pushes down on the inside half to begin the separation.

7. To make a low, platelike lid, center the clay on a rather wide base. With thumbs locked together try to feel the curve and slowly, in two or three pulls, work the clay outward.

8. Watch both the inside and the outside as the curve develops. When excess clay must be trimmed away, hold the needle in a nearly vertical position and support the wall from underneath.

9. Calipers verify the diameter using the measurement taken in fig. 6. The lid may be cut now with a wire or allowed to separate later from the bat.

or slapping the clay is necessary to produce certain heavy textures. Whenever possible, these should be imprinted before the rim is divided. Texturing the pot afterward is apt to knock the lip fatally off-center.

Whether a finger, an eraser, or some other tool is used to force the ledge downward, it should be pushed to a good depth. Containers of this kind look better if the lid is seated rather deeply so that the edge of the lid is not visible above the edge of the jar itself. Also, if the ledge is scarcely below the rim of the jar, the lid is more likely to be dislodged accidentally.

A knob thrown directly on the trimmed lid could have been used rather than a pulled handle. This technique may be seen on pages 48–49. While the two forms were being made, the wheel was spinning at an average-to-fast speed; it was slowed down somewhat for making the platelike lid.

4. The eraser of a pencil or some similar tool may be used to start the division and to push the ledge deeper. The tool must be held steady to keep the ledge and lip spinning on center.

5. As the ledge is completed, the lip is finished off with a bevel. Use a finger pad to curve the ledge up into the lip. The slight curve will allow the lid some play.

6. A measurement for the lid should be taken immediately after throwing is completed. Hold the reversed calipers so that the tips touch the midpoints of the ledge.

10. Because the bat did not dry the bottom of the lid quickly enough, a fettling knife was slipped between the two to speed the separation.

11. When trimming a lid with a simple curve, such as the one shown here, it is often helpful to use the flat edge of a flexible metal rib; bend it to increase contact with the surface of the clay.

12. The form was completed with a section of a pulled handle. It was laid over a broomstick and allowed to harden for about an hour before being attached to the lid.

SHOULDER LID

A shoulder lid makes an effective cover for jars and containers of widely varied form. To serve a decorative or useful purpose, a knob or handle may be attached, although as long as the lid is no wider than the hand's grasp, none is needed. Indeed, one of the most satisfying aspects of this lid and container combination may be its sculptural character—perhaps more emphatic without a knob or handle than with one. But unless one or the other is to be used, a shallow, domed lid should

1. During lifting, when an essentially vertical form is desired, try to prevent the clay from widening at the top. To accomplish this, encircle the piece evenly with both hands and then squeeze inward.

2. A ridge has been started. Pressure from the inside hand pushes the clay outward and forces it between the index and middle fingers of the right hand.

3. The form has been collared in once more and is nearing its final shape. Here the ridge is being given sharper definition between the fingertips of both hands.

7. To remove such a form, wet the half of the wheelhead nearest you with water or thin slip. Tilt the pot backward and slide it onto a tile or board covered with wet paper.

8. To throw the cover, brace your hands, keep your arms at your sides, and slowly pull the wall toward you until it is vertical. Pulling laterally, in opposite directions, can quickly throw the clay off-center.

9. The cover has been thrown wide at the top to correspond to the slant of the collar. Here, the bevelled edge, which will rest on the shoulder, is being formed by the index finger.

be avoided, particularly if a smooth, shiny glaze is being considered. With nothing to grab hold of, the fingers will keep slipping off the glassy surface.

Do not throw a high collar on the container unless you want an even higher lid, for the lid should be tall enough to clear the collar-edge and reach the shoulder; otherwise, it will seem to float and will not be seated securely.

The measurement for the lid should be marked on paper and kept in a safe place. In that way, if the lid gets broken before firing, another one can be made. Without the measurement one must often guess at the correct diameter, because the container will have dried and shrunk.

4. Extra clay was left at the top to conclude the form. A shoulder is begun by holding the fingers at a 45-degree angle and pressing the clay against the supporting left hand.

5. As the diameter of the opening diminishes, the wall becomes thicker, thus providing, in this case, enough clay to lift a collar which will help to hold the lid in place.

6. Calipers measure the diameter at the point where the shoulder merges into the collar. This measurement should be transferred to a piece of paper and kept in a safe place.

10. If the measurements are recorded, a broken lid can be made again even after a pot has been fired. The calipers compare the inner diameter with the one taken from the jar.

11. Now leather-hard, the cover is trimmed. So as not to cut through or weaken the form when bevelling the edge, you must leave the cover rounded on the inside during throwing.

12. The cover is small enough to be lifted quite easily. It does not rest on the lip of the jar—only on the shoulder.

LID WITH THROWN KNOB

Without the knob this lid could almost serve as a bowl, differing only in proportion from the tall, flaring form made earlier (pages 28–29). To begin the lid, the clay is centered on a narrow base and is somewhat taller than usual. After a hole has been pushed into the mass in the normal V shape, there is no further opening. The knuckle strongly undercuts the base and starts the clay moving diagonally upward and outward.

All potters are occasionally disappointed and annoyed when they find that a lid does not fit its container.

1. Keep your arms against your body. The hands work as a unit when joined by the left thumb. With steady pressure lift the clay gradually and the finger rings will be equidistantly spaced.

2. While shaping a form, the tips of the fingers cause less friction and give finer control than the knuckle. Here the clay is being pushed outward and a ledge is being created for the lid.

3. To flare the lip to this diameter, the lid must be left thicker at the top during lifting. Experimentation with finger positions is necessary to find what lip forms are possible.

7. When completed, the lid will have a wide-based, conical shape. It must be started correctly. Undercut the clay strongly with the knuckle and begin moving the hands outward at a 45-degree angle.

8. There is no interior floor. The walls fan out from the point of the cone. With interlocked thumbs, the fingers guide and shape the clay. The right hand is supporting the wall from beneath.

9. If too much clay has been used, trim the excess with a needle before the lid becomes too flat. Use as little water as possible when throwing a form this extended.

Inaccurate measuring can be responsible, of course, but assuming care was taken, there are other reasons why the lid may end up too large or too small. If a very soft clay is used to throw the lid and a stiff clay, the jar, the lid, containing more water, will shrink more when it dries. To overcome this problem, throw both forms from the same piece of wedged clay. Also, if it takes ten minutes to get the ledge and lid of a jar just right, using quantities of water all the while, and the lid comes just right immediately, then expect that the two forms may not fit properly when finally dry. With experience, one learns to compensate in these instances by making the lid a bit wider or narrower as the case may be.

The finished lid and jar may be seen together in the next section.

4. A pronounced ledge is needed to permit the cover to rest level and not tilt. The measurement being taken by the inverted calipers will be marked on paper and used for the lid.

5. This jar will remain flat on the bottom, with the distinctive whorls left by the cutting wire. The only trimming necessary—a slightly bevelled undercut—is completed now.

6. The cylinder arches out to support the ledge. A right-angled, overhanging ledge may collapse while being made or during firing. Keep the wire taut and pressed against the wheelhead.

10. The lid was eased out to the correct diameter and given a strong, rounded lip. A diameter slightly less than that of the ledge will afford the lid some play and prevent it from binding.

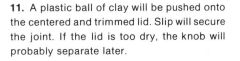

11. A plastic ball of clay will be pushed onto the centered and trimmed lid. Slip will secure the joint. If the lid is too dry, the knob will probably separate later.

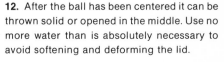

12. After the ball has been centered it can be thrown solid or opened in the middle. Use no more water than is absolutely necessary to avoid softening and deforming the lid.

FLAT INSET LID

The flat inset lid can be thrown on the wheelhead, but there are disadvantages to making it that way. It is difficult to get a wire beneath the clay without slicing into the edge; and, once cut free, the lid cannot easily be removed unless it is given time to stiffen. When an absolutely flat lid is not required, the edges can be lifted a bit with a modelling tool. This is shown being done on page 68, fig. 8. When the lid is thrown this way, the edges can be finished on both sides and the wire passed safely beneath the form. If a completely flat lid is desired, make

1. This photograph is included again to place it in the proper sequence. Taking the measurement for the lid should be done immediately after the jar has been thrown.

2. Paddle a ball of clay into a pancake form before beginning to center. The left hand curves over the edge and pushes inward. The right hand presses downward and levels the mass.

3. A mound is left in the center. Beyond it the clay is depressed further and moved toward the outer edge. A sponge is used to make a smoother surface.

7. To use the entire plaster surface, you must center the bat almost perfectly. The calipers show this diameter to be approximately 1/8 inch too large.

8. A vertical cut is made 1/16 inch in from the edge. When trimming with the needle steadiness is critical. Practice frequently on pieces that will not be kept to gain facility and confidence.

9. After the correct diameter has been cut, the edge of the lid can be finished with a suitable wooden tool. The upper surface of the lid will not be disturbed during trimming.

it in one of two ways: on a bat so that it does not need cutting and can be left to break free as it was thrown; or, off the hump, a method described in a later chapter (pages 74–75).

It is customary to fire lid and container together to prevent warping and distortion, particularly of the container's rim. Since a flat lid may be susceptible to sagging when being fired, if a lid much wider than the one shown here is used, it may sag or collapse when in the kiln. For that reason, when making a form with a wide mouth such as a large casserole, a curved inset lid is more practical to use than a flat one.

The interchangeability of several different lids and containers should be considered. For example, the two lids shown here could be used with the jar shown on pages 44–45 and the curved inset lid accompanying that form could be used to cover the jar pictured below.

4. A needle should be employed frequently and at several points to test the thickness of the clay. Since nothing will be lost to the cutting wire, 1/4 inch is a suitable thickness.

5. The center mound will be used to throw a knob for the lid. With the fingers encircling the form, it is pushed inward to a smaller diameter.

6. Thrown hollow, the knob is formed by slowly forcing one finger into the clay and lifting and shaping it as one would a mini-cylinder. Excessive finger pressure will twist the wall.

10. Little remains to be done after the form has separated from the bat. While the lid rests loosely on a chuck, a special or makeshift container for trimming, the clay burr on the edge is removed.

11. Lids and jars are often allowed to dry together. A safer method is to dry each form separately on a flat surface, with the jar placed upside-down.

12. This is the lid thrown previously. Although the jar was given two covers to illustrate different methods of forming, having a variety of lids to choose from is usually advantageous.

The flanged lid is one of the most versatile of the covers. Like the curved inset and the shoulder lid, it is thrown upside down. It can rest on a vertical or curved wall (fig. 12), or be used on a container with an inside ledge (pages 44–45). When intended for the latter use, the lid must be measured in two places: the diameter of the flange (corresponding to the opening of the container) and the diameter of the outer edge (corresponding to the diameter of the ledge).

A flanged lid may be made in many different sizes.

1. For control, keep the left thumb braced against the right hand while the cylinder is being lifted. To facilitate raising the wall, the inside fingertips have undercut the clay at the base.

2. Held in a curve, the fingertips of the right hand act as a template and force the wall inward. Position yourself to watch the form develop.

3. To give a plain, rounded form to the lip, a chamois strip or an elephant ear sponge (which is being used here) may be folded over the rim and pressed lightly.

7. The vertical flange was trimmed to reduce its height. Its diameter, measured at the line of the plane change should be slightly less than that of the container opening.

8. The trimming tool chosen will cut very clear rings. Since the lip was formed on both sides during throwing, it will not require any cutting.

9. Study the inside curve and the clay thickness before beginning to trim. Rather than run the risk of cutting through the top, take off the clay lugs and examine the lid again.

When thrown smaller than the one illustrated on these pages, it can be grasped and lifted without a knob or handle. The teapots shown on pages 56–57, 59, and 84–85, contain such lids. Its form is particularly suited to teapots because the flange can be thrown to the length needed to hold it inside the pot while tea is being poured. On pages 76–77, a much larger flanged lid can be seen, one which covers a casserole and is lifted with a pulled handle.

Throwing this type of lid involves some guesswork,

but here are two rules of thumb: first, during shaping, bring the wall to a diameter approximately that of the opening of the container; second, keep the rim, which will be split into a lip and flange, a double thickness. Without the extra clay it will not be possible to give the lid the sturdy edges it needs to avoid being chipped when in use.

4. The opening is measured for a flanged lid and a recessed lid. If one postpones taking this measurement, the lid will be too small because the opening will have begun to shrink as it dries.

5. To make a flanged lid, center the clay in a low form and open it with a flat or curved floor. When the rim is approximately the diameter of the jar opening, divide it and push the outer half downward.

6. Decide how far the lip of the lid is to extend beyond the edge of the jar, and trim any excess with a needle. This illustration shows the lip, already trimmed, being shaped and rounded.

10. Two clay strips were pulled and then laid over a quart jar to become firm. A paper towel was used to keep the clay from sticking to the glass.

11. Do not feel committed to the curve of a quart jar. When the clay is firm, it will still be plastic enough to allow the handle to be shaped in many other ways.

12. Avoid making the lid flange a vertical form. It can bind when inside or while entering the jar. Rather, the flange should slant to a slightly smaller diameter at its finished edge.

RECESSED LID

Another versatile cover is the recessed lid. Like the flanged lid, it may be used on a plain lip, such as the pot on this page contains, or set on an inside ledge. It, too, works well on teapots (page 58), its socket holding it inside during pouring. Easier to throw than the flanged lid, it can be started in a similar manner with a centered lump whose diameter equals that of the container opening. A knob is not a necessity; the center mound can be eliminated and a pulled loop used in its place.

1. The shape of the clay when centered may still be seen. Its diameter approximates that of the container opening (page 53, fig. 4). Open the mass off center, leaving enough to make a knob.

2. The center mound has been pushed inward to begin the knob. Having been drawn open, the clay is now being lifted, thinned, and given an outward flare at the lip.

3. Excess clay on the socket, the bowl-like underpart, was shaved off with a modelling tool. The knob is shown being undercut with a finger and lifted into an open, flaring form.

4. The flange of the lid must be flat enough to rest level on the lip of the container. Measure directly beneath the flange (not on the bat) at the point where the planes change.

5. Almost no trimming is necessary. A knife blade passed around the edge can smooth it; or, the form can be trimmed in a chuck. Open-mouth forms that are leather-hard, bisqued, or glazed may be used as chucks.

6. Like the flanged lid shown previously, the recessed lid should be thrown with a curve or taper inward at the base to prevent binding.

TEAPOT I
SIDE HANDLE

It is difficult to make a good teapot, one of the most complex forms the potter contends with. Several technical problems must be solved if the teapot is to function well, and the parts themselves must be harmoniously adjusted to one another. In addition the components must be made with a view to their assembly and kept the proper consistency so that handle and knob may be attached successfully, and neither spout nor teapot becomes too dry for the other. When finally assembled, the form needs special attention during drying. It may

1. The teapot form was begun as a simple cylinder. A somewhat thicker wall in the middle enables the curve to be widely distended without undue thinning.

2. A small lump of clay is opened somewhat like the knob of a lid. The fingers work together, touching each other for support when possible. Keep the clay slanting inward.

3. Starting at the bottom and moving up the sides, the fingertips steady the rising form and begin to shape it. Finger pressure must be equal on both sides or the clay may twist and break.

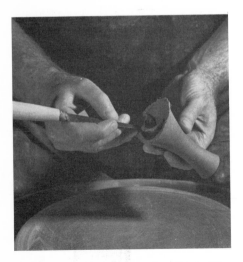

7. When the spout becomes firm, thin out the lower wall with a fettling knife. A thickness of 1/8 inch, plus or minus, is adequate.

8. Before cutting the spout to fit the teapot, hold it in several positions against the wall to find the best placement. Tea will flow out if the spout opening is too low.

9. After the spout has been cut to fit the teapot, its outline is used to determine where to place the strainer holes. These should be rather large and kept well inside the area scored for the spout.

be necessary to wrap the handle and the spout to prevent their cracking.

It will help in visualizing the final form to make some sketches before starting: what kind of lid to use, where to place the spout, the size and curve of the handle, etc.

The following practical considerations are important yet frequently overlooked. The pouring lip of the spout should be near the level of the rim; otherwise tea will flow out before the pot is filled. Pouring holes should be large enough to allow a free flow of liquid and placed high enough on the pot to escape being clogged with leaves. The handle should be attached directly opposite the spout and should balance the teapot, particularly when it is filled. A side handle looks best when placed on a flat or concave form. A fully rounded pot usually looks better with an overhead handle.

4. If the clay is worked only on the outside, the spout-wall will not thin out properly. A finger must be kept inside the rising spout form as long as possible for thinning and controlling the shape.

5. A flanged lid has been made and trimmed. The flange is tall to keep the lid from falling out when the pot is tilted. A taper at the bottom will prevent the lid from binding.

6. Making accessory forms gives one a choice. It is not necessary to make all the parts at the same time. However, those chosen should have the same moisture content when finally assembled.

10. Both forms are scored and slipped before being assembled. Here a thin coil of clay is run along the seam to strengthen the joint.

11. The spout, shown here being trimmed of unwanted clay, has been kept moist enough so that a pouring lip (similar to that made for a pitcher) is easily pulled out with a finger.

12. If the lid fits snugly—and it should—it is necessary to cut an air-intake hole to prevent hot liquid from being forced out the spout. Be sure the hole is started inside the lid flange.

When an overhead handle is attached to what seemed a modest form, it can be disconcerting suddenly to find a giant pot looming up. Consider the fact that an overhead handle may increase the teapot's height by one-quarter to one-third. Unless the handle is a good height, however, it becomes an annoying chore to lift out and replace the lid without bumping into and perhaps breaking one of the two forms. The socket or flange of the chosen lid should be deep enough to hold it inside when the teapot is tilted for pouring.

1. A good grip on the clay and steady inward pressure collars the form. As the diameter of the top lessens, the wall thickens and more clay becomes available for the upper area.

2. A recessed lid will cover the teapot. Center an amount of clay whose base is approximately equal to the diameter of the teapot opening. A deep valley divides the socket from the knob.

3. While throwing, check the thickness of the floor. Raise the wall sufficiently to form a deep socket which will hold the lid inside the teapot during pouring.

4. If the diameter were much smaller, the pot would be too unstable to trim upside down without a chuck. A wooden modeling tool is being used to smooth the clay surface after trimming.

5. Two handles of different cross section have been pulled, cut from the cone, and draped over a large pickle jar. Thirty minutes to one hour will be enough to harden them.

6. An overhead handle and a spout, left untrimmed on the end, complete the form. Attach the handle while it has some play so that the curve can be adjusted, if necessary, without cracking the clay.

TEAPOT III
BAMBOO HANDLE

Bamboo handles may be purchased from ceramic suppliers in a variety of styles and sizes. Also, many hobby shops sell dry cane, a material which can easily be bent into a handle form after being softened in water. The cane ends are then split in half and curved to form loops. After insertion into the clay lugs, the loops are whipped shut. If the bamboo handle is a bit too small or too large for the fired teapot, it, too, can be soaked in water and then stretched or compressed to fit the teapot lugs.

1. Two fingers push a small concavity into the clay to form the shoulder needed for the handle lugs. In teapots and pitchers a thin, even wall is very desirable.

2. When thinning the clay for a teapot spout, one finger must be kept inside as long as possible. To avoid twisting the wall, lift slowly and keep the fingers moving vertically.

3. When the wall has been properly thinned, a final taper or curvature can be given to the spout by a light fingertip-collaring. Start at the base and work upward, applying equal pressure to both sides.

4. The under edge of the flanged lid, which will rest on the teapot lip, is levelled with a stick. Cut or drill an air-intake hole into the clay when the lid becomes leather-hard.

5. Two small coils are attached to the shoulder. These coil-lugs must be positioned to allow ample clearance for the lid when the handle is in place.

6. Although the bamboo handle is too narrow now, the teapot will shrink to fit it during firing. Unless they are wrapped with plastic, the lugs may dry too quickly and crack.

59

COMPOTE I

A compote is a footed bowl from which fruits and other edibles may be served. The foot and the bowl should remain strong forms visually even as they unite in a new entity. Set the bowl on the foot. If the foot seems too prominent, it can be trimmed shorter before attachment. Set the foot on the bowl. Spin the wheel and be as certain as possible that the base is level. If it is not, move the foot until it is. An off-center foot will cause a lopsided pot which may deform drastically during firing.

1. All excess clay has been cut from the bowl and the inner and outer curves match exactly. Several circles are inscribed on the form to guide the placement of the foot.

2. A foot had been made earlier from a sketch and has now reached the consistency of the bowl. Making the foot upside down allows the base to be thrown rather than trimmed.

3. The foot has been righted and carefully centered. It must be given a level edge as an aid to correct placement on the bowl. The bevel will be cut to match the bowl's curvature.

4. After testing the two forms for a good fit and being certain that the foot is level, the surfaces to be joined are roughened and slipped before attachment.

5. Place the foot accurately and press it firmly for a good bond. Run a small coil around the exterior and interior seams and smooth them with a modeling tool or a fingertip while the wheel turns.

6. Spin the wheel. If the bowl is lopsided, the foot should be cut off and repositioned. The safest way to dry the compote is upside down on a perfectly level surface.

COMPOTE II
THROWING A COIL

There are advantages to using a preformed foot for the compote, as was done in the preceding section. A very tall one can be thrown at one sitting, making a neat, tidy package ready for assembly. Or, several with different dimensions can be prepared so that a selection may be made. There are disadvantages, too. Thrown apart from the bowl, the foot may never be exactly what is needed—too thin, too wide, not quite the right taper, etc. And the problem of centering a preformed foot, of getting it level on the bowl, is by no means automatically

1. From a well-wedged piece of clay take a good-sized lump and squeeze it as evenly as possible into a heavy ropelike form.

2. Lightly roll the clay beneath open hands. A surface which is level and somewhat absorbent is best to use. The coil will develop more evenly when the hands move apart from the center outward.

3. Thick and thin spots may begin to develop. Paddle a thick section with the fingers to help thin it. A thin spot can be thickened by rolling toward it from the ends.

7. Wiggle the coil on the slipped surface to help secure the joint. This illustration shows the clay being welded to the bowl. Give the inside seam the same treatment.

8. If the diameter of the coil varies considerably, the wall will soon become thick and thin and go off center. Throw as dry as possible to avoid softening and perhaps collapsing the bowl.

9. Several cuts with the needle may be required to level the edge and give the foot the desired height. Keep the form somewhat heavier than usual. It must support the weight of the bowl above it.

solved.

Using a coil to make a foot can overcome some of these difficulties (although a few new ones are substituted). When a coil is thrown, one has an opportunity to see the foot develop and to adjust its form and proportion. The process is more organic. Also, when finally trimmed with a needle, the foot is level and parallel to the plane of the bowl rim. The disadvantages or, more accurately, the difficulties, are technical in nature: the coil must be correctly prepared; it must be exactly cen-

tered and kept on center during throwing. The possibility exists, too, that the weight of the coil may collapse the bowl, particularly if an excess of water is used.

Using a coil which is thrown on the pot has numerous applications and the potter can make many forms other than a foot. Some of these are shown in subsequent sections.

4. When the clay has been rolled to the desired diameter, form a ring and smash the ends together. A good seal is absolutely essential.

5. The joint must be smoothed until it has the same diameter as the rest of the coil. If a fat joint is left, it will bump the wall off center every time it hits the fingers during throwing.

6. The coil must be centered exactly on the trimmed bowl. Mark a pencil line where the foot will begin. Then hold the pencil against the spinning coil to see if it has been placed correctly.

10. A trimming tool removes excess clay at the joint. If it were decided at this stage to make a taller foot, the rim could be dried awhile and another coil added to it exactly as before.

11. The wall is flared slightly and the foot rim given a sturdy form. Compacting the clay is important—it may keep the rim from going out-of-round during firing.

12. Large bowls warp readily when being fired. Changing the direction of the form at the lip strengthens the bowl and lessens this tendency as does drying the rim carefully on a flat surface.

BOTTLE I

A cylinder is thrown to begin. It may be proportioned in any way. Experience will tell you what range of bottle forms is possible from any given cylinder and, conversely, what kind of cylinder is necessary to make a particular bottle.

Do not push the clay wall out too quickly. Take two or three lifts to shape the curve. The curve and the pot's inner space are steadily changing, and unless the potter watches them carefully, he may miss a pleasing form, unaware that it has developed. Forming the bottle's

1. Keep the clay collared in. The cylinder will be forced out to a near-spherical form, and to provide the necessary clay, the wall must be kept somewhat thicker than usual.

2. Starting at the base, the inside hand begins to push the clay into a gradual arc. Lean immediately to one side to see clearly the developing form.

3. A wooden rib (in this case a tongue depressor) may be used in place of the fingertips or knuckle to steady the wall and form the curve. Move the clay outward gradually.

7. More clay is available than will be used, so the top is trimmed and levelled. If a very tall neck is wanted, do not cut off so much clay at this time.

8. The neck is collared in again. With thumbs and fingers try to support and constrict the rather fragile clay wall so that it does not twist or break apart.

9. A finger on the inside of the bottle must now work with the outside hand to give a final form to the shoulder and its area of transition with the neck.

neck often gives the most trouble. One must alternate between squeezing the clay in, which thickens it, and lifting the wall to thin it out. Until you are near the end, keep the opening no larger than is needed to put a hand inside, because if the top flares out too far, it cannot be brought back in without rippling and twisting. Collaring, a compressive use of the hands, can counter outward movement and force the clay into a smaller diameter.

Use water sparingly; thin slip may be used in its place. If the pot gets too wet, it may collapse at the shoulder. If water has been left inside the form after the neck is constricted, tie a small piece of sponge to a stick and insert it into the bottle to remove the liquid.

As a last resort if the shoulder caves in, the clay can be trimmed and the form allowed to sit awhile. A small coil can then be attached and thrown to conclude the form.

4. The fingers begin to shape the shoulder. Too much pressure downward may collapse the curve which must be supported from the inside. Leave a collar of clay at the top to form the neck.

5. The fingers of both hands encircle the clay and give steady, even support as the wall is squeezed into a smaller diameter. When strong pressure is being applied, release the hands slowly.

6. As the neck narrows, the clay thickens. It is then lifted and thinned out like any cylinder. Do not let the top flare out or it may ripple when forced back in.

10. The neck is shaped and the lip given a bevel. This form and the teapot spout are thrown similarly, the hand positions being much the same. The wheel slows in the final stages.

11. Now is a good time to cut away unwanted clay from the lower wall. This will refine the contour and lessen the bottle's weight. No further trimming should be necessary.

12. Press the cut-off wire down on the wheelhead so it does not cut up into the bottle. When the clay has firmed, the bottom can be tapped in at the center to counteract a possible drying bulge.

BOTTLE II
Throwing with Sections

Using sections enables one to throw a tall form more easily than it could be thrown from a single lump of clay. The technique is a flexible one and open to variation and combination with other methods of working. For example, two or more completed sections can be thrown separately and then assembled when the clay is firm. The compote of page 61 was made in sections and so could vases, jars, and other tall forms. A variant might entail throwing two or more sections to a predetermined size, joining them, and then continuing the form to con-

1. The section on the wheelhead was thrown last and has become firm. It must support the weight of the other cylinder, which was covered and kept softer.

2. A thick, flat lip was left on both forms to provide a substantial area of contact when the halves are assembled. A comb is a useful tool for quickly scoring edges.

3. Proper clay consistency is a critical factor. If the cylinders are too wet, twisting may occur or the bottom form may buckle. If the clay is too dry, further shaping will be difficult.

7. A minimum of water should be used during throwing. The center area has been wet lightly, and inward pressure from a wooden rib begins to smooth the joint.

8. Most of the water used will probably be applied to the upper half which will need softening and thinning. Here the clay is being collared in to a smaller diameter.

9. Shaping continues on the upper section. All traces of the joint have been smoothed away with a rib and the form is slowly being distended to its final dimensions.

clusion with a coil or two. Or again, coil-throwing could for some reason be sandwiched between two preformed sections.

The method illustrated here assumes the potter has made some decisions regarding the final form. It is to be a bottle, a vase, a pitcher, etc., of a rather definite proportion. One may, of course, always discover something different en route, but it would probably be a form in the context of the sections being used.

To begin, two stable sections, chosen for their simi-larity to the envisioned final form, are thrown with the same top diameter. Throw the one that is to go on top first, so that the bottom section can remain centered on the wheelhead or a bat. Although it is conceivable that a globe could be made from two wide cones, the method lends itself more readily to tall, narrow forms.

4. Slip was used between the edges. Accurate positioning of the top form is essential, otherwise throwing will be almost impossible. Jiggle the upper cylinder to effect a stronger joint.

5. The bottom of the upper form is now cut out. Keep the wheel spinning and hold a pencil point against the top section. If it is not aligned, separate and reposition the halves.

6. Before starting to throw the sections, strengthen the joint by pushing clay over the seams. The inside should be similarly treated. Avoid pushing the top form off center.

10. The bottom has been worked, too. As inward pressure develops the shoulder, the wall thickens and clay is provided for the neck and the lip.

11. The neck must be formed by a combination of collaring and lifting and thinning. If the clay becomes so wet or so thin that a twist or break seems imminent, let it sit for fifteen minutes.

12. While a form is being thrown, a conscious decision is often made regarding the clay surface. Finger-rings may be wanted or a smoother treatment may seem more desirable.

GOBLET

There are several interesting ways to make the handleless, long-stemmed drinking cup called a goblet. Two of these methods involve techniques which have already been described. Reduce a compote, one with a spacious bowl and a tall foot, to a size which can be lifted in one hand and used to drink from, and you have a goblet. In fact, the goblet can be made like a compote with a preformed foot which is slipped onto the bowl when both are leather-hard. It can also be made with a coil that is set into position on the trimmed bowl and

1. Center a small ball of clay whose diameter is close to that of the desired goblet base. Divide the form near the outer edge, leaving a sizable amount of clay in the middle.

2. With fingers and thumbs around the column of clay, press inward and lift at the same time. Lifting too rapidly can quickly twist the shaft off center.

3. Press in harder to narrow the stem. Once the clay has begun to assume a more definite form, the edge of a flexible rib may be useful in establishing a clean profile.

7. If the top is not level, a final trim with the needle is essential. Here a fingertip is forming the concavity into which the goblet cup will be placed.

8. A wooden tool is being used to lift the edge of the base and smooth its under-surface. A wire may then cut the form free without damaging the finished edge.

9. If a sketch of the goblet has not already been made, it would be helpful to visualize or put on paper a tentative relationship of the two forms before starting the cup.

thrown to the desired height. Both of these methods have the advantages and disadvantages already mentioned.

The third method, a variation of the second, also produces a hollow-stemmed goblet. Take a golfball of clay and attach it to the bottom of the trimmed bowl, welding the edges with care. Figs. 11 and 12, page 49, show this technique being employed. The small clay ball is then opened with a fingertip and thrown into a foot two to three inches in height.

The method illustrated in these photographs gives a solid-stemmed form—one that has to a degree the elegance of a glass goblet. Indeed, some potters see the resemblance to glass as being too great and therefore indicative of a method of working which does not exploit the special nature of clay. The suggestion made when the compote-foot was attached bears repeating: be certain that the stem is level so that the goblet will not be lopsided.

4. Pushing inward with the fingertips has undercut the clay and created a bulbous form near the bottom of the stem. A needle now reduces the diameter of the base and removes unwanted clay.

5. The index finger thins the base, drawing clay toward the outer edge. Keep track of the thickness with a needle.

6. The stem (and other thin, solid forms like it) tend to wobble off center rather easily. Hold it firmly, supporting as much of the curve as possible with the fingertips.

10. The small base from which the cup was begun (fig 9) has been steadily reduced by undercutting. Its remains can be seen on the wheelhead after excess clay was shaved away.

11. At the leather-hard stage the clay was trimmed again—nearly to a point. Inscribe a circle on the cup as a guide for the placement of the stem.

12. Look at the forms together before attaching them. If they seem unsuited to one another, there are two alternatives: throw additional parts or trim the stem lower.

DOUGHNUT

When left as thrown, the doughnut is a strong, visually powerful, three-dimensional form. It has often been used in historical and contemporary ceramics, whole or in sections, to make sculptures and a variety of utilitarian forms. Stood vertically, it has been opened at the top, given a foot, and thereby turned into a bottle or a vase. Laid flat, it has been fitted with vertical stems and utilized as a lamp or a candleholder. Doughnut sections comprise parts of vases; they have been used to make teapot handles and decorative elements of other pots.

1. When you begin a doughnut, the normal floor thickness is not needed. But leave a thin skin on the wheelhead, otherwise the clay ring may break loose while being opened.

2. The solid doughnut of fig. 1 needs to be hollowed. The first step involves splitting the clay into equal halves by pushing the fingers into the middle of the spinning ring. Hold steady to maintain the centering.

3. Although the center hole of the doughnut will not be used, be sure to leave a normal thickness of clay at the bottom of the two walls—1/4-3/8 inch should be adequate.

7. When the edges meet, the clay settles a bit and the top rounds off. Give the seam careful attention with fingers or a rib to avoid having it open later.

8. Scrap clay from the center hole has been removed. This photograph shows the clay that was in contact with the wheelhead—perhaps two thirds of the diameter of the ring.

9. Trim accurately to match the curvature of the thrown area. The doughnut may be used as thrown in sculptures and numerous utilitarian forms.

The doughnut is indeed a serviceable and versatile form.

The first time a doughnut is attempted, it may end up oval in section rather than round. To overcome this, the two curving walls must be formed symmetrically, each a semicircle, and made to meet in the center, a bit higher than necessary. When the edges are pushed together, with pressure inward and downward on the joint, the form should become round. If the clay was not split into two equal parts, one wall will be too short and a round section will be more difficult to achieve.

A template may be used to check the roundness of the doughnut section while the form is being made. Take a square of cardboard and cut a slightly flat semicircle out of one side. Set this cutout on the wheelhead and push it up against the curve. Use it on the other wall, too.

4. Start lifting the inner wall first. After thinning the clay, curve it to a nearly semicircular form. The bottom must curve, too, and merge gradually into the arc of the wall.

5. To arrive at a doughnut form whose cross section is a true circle, each wall must be accurately curved. Here the outer wall is thinned and lifted to the proper height.

6. The curve of each side was thrown slightly flat with each wall a bit higher than necessary. Here the lips, left a good thickness, are slowly forced together from the outside.

10. To alter the doughnut in this way—reducing the diameter and pulling the edges apart—the clay must be just short of leatherhard. If too dry, it will crack or open at the seam.

11. The diameter of the section was taken after throwing was completed. Two cylinders of the same measurement, one with a finished lip, will be added to the open ends.

12. Thrown somewhat taller than required, the two cylinders have been trimmed and attached to the ends of the doughnut, which will be used as a candleholder.

HORS D'OEUVRES TRAY

Splitting the opened ring off center may lead to some unusual and unexpected forms. In addition to the hors d'oeuvres tray, a number of other utilitarian pieces can be thrown when the inside wall is the thicker of the two. One example is an orange juice squeezer. If that form is made, the wall of the cone should be left somewhat heavier than usual so that flutings can be carved into it when the clay is leather-hard.

When the outside wall is thicker, equally interesting forms may be developed. Still other possibilities exist

1. The clay mass has just been opened on a large bat. While the inside fingertips undercut the wall, the edge of the right hand levels and compresses the rim.

2. Although the doughnut ring was split into halves, this ring will be divided off center. Since more clay will be needed for the inside wall, the cut is being made nearer the outside edge.

3. Test the thickness of the floor with a needle. With the inside fingers tucked into the undercut, the hands are in position to lift the wall inward.

7. Continuing pressure at the neck finally pinched the clay shut. After the lifting knob had been concluded, it seemed as if that form was too small and too thin.

8. Not enough clay was available near the top of the cone to reopen the neck and throw another knob. Therefore, the small form was pinched off.

9. The tray was allowed to dry until nearly leather-hard. To form a new knob, a lump of plastic clay is being pushed onto the cone-tip and welded into place.

when the ring is divided into three parts. One then has an inner, outer, and middle wall to work with. Coils may be added to one or all of the walls so that the form can be enlarged well beyond the size available from the original ring. The use of preformed parts further increases the range of possibility. The next chapter contains several suggestions for altering wheel pieces. Some of the ideas mentioned there are applicable to working with the ring form.

Whichever way the clay is divided, be sure to brace the

fingers (fig. 2) when pushing into the ring. If centering is lost at this point, it will be almost impossible to lift and shape the clay.

4. Equality of pressure from the hands holds the form on center during the collaring process. The index fingers riding on the lip help to level and thicken it.

5. The diameter of the cone at its base has been reduced to provide more tray space. The clay is still being lifted, thinned, and forced inward.

6. At this stage the conical form must be thrown like a bottle. Supported evenly by fingers and thumbs, the walls are gradually eased into a point.

10. A lump this size may seem difficult to center. Put ten fingertips around it and hold them steady. While the knob is being shaped, work the clay together carefully at the joint.

11. The second knob is larger, sturdier looking, and more in scale with the rest of the form. It will be a comfortable handle for lifting and carrying the tray.

12. A two-gallon glaze crock makes a convenient chuck for trimming certain larger forms. In this case the tray's own weight holds it steady.

THROWING OFF THE HUMP

To anyone who has had difficulty centering a softball-sized lump of clay, the manipulation of the "hump" may seem forbidding. Actually, the large mass can be brought to a rough center rather quickly by slamming it onto the stationary wheelhead and pounding and slapping it into a tapering form. Then, as the wheel spins rapidly, the clay can be lifted into a cone by an encircling, upward pressure of the hands.

Throwing off the hump can be a time- and energy-saving method of making a quantity of small forms—

1. Before turning the wheel, paddle a large lump of clay into approximate symmetry. Then, with the wheel spinning rapidly, squeeze the clay upward into a cone and steady the top as shown here.

2. The entire mass need not be perfectly centered. Attention is given to the top where a small amount of clay is pressed inward, steadied and opened to begin a cup.

3. The pot has been completed and the point of a trimming stick is used to mark a line into the undercut area—about 1/4 inch beneath the floor of the form.

7. The severed cup is lifted off the hump to be set aside to dry. The cone top will now be drawn up and centered again in preparation for throwing another form.

8. A lid can be thrown from the hump provided it is kept rather dry and the diameter is not too great. Here a flat inset lid is being drawn out and given a strong undercut.

9. A kitchen spatula will be used to cut the lid from the hump. Throw with as little water as possible and the lid will be less apt to deform during removal.

74

cups, mugs, goblet bowls, etc. It eliminates the need for centering individually each small lump of clay. When a pot has been cut off, by one of the two methods illustrated, the remaining flat top must again be pushed into a cone before the next pot is begun. As one establishes a rhythm of centering, opening, and shaping, the small forms, often parts of sets, can be thrown with freedom and verve.

The three most common problems involve removal. First, be sure to cut the proper distance beneath the pot so the bottom is neither cut out nor left too thick and heavy. Second, use water sparingly so the pot may be more easily lifted from the mound. Third, avoid making pots which are too large or too delicate to remove without deformation—forms which should be made in the usual manner on a bat or the wheelhead.

4. The pot will be cut free with a piece of household string. The wheel has been stopped and the string is being placed in the line so that the form can be cut off horizontally.

5. The wheel begins to turn very slowly while the string, held securely in the right hand, is drawn taut and allowed to run entirely around the base of the pot.

6. The wheel continues slowly. After the string has made one revolution, it is given a light tug backward and immediately the pot is cut free.

10. The spatula is wet with water and held horizontally against the undercut. Cut near enough to the lid so that the bottom will not require extensive trimming.

11. With the wheel spinning at moderate speed, a slight but firm pressure of the spatula will cut the lid free and slide it onto the wet blade.

12. Care must be taken when lifting these small, wet forms whether from the spatula or from the hump itself. Hold them at the base where the clay is firm and thicker.

CASSEROLE

A casserole is a covered dish or bowl, often a large one. Since its purpose is for cooking food in an oven and later for serving, its form should reflect that double function. It tends to be wide and not too tall, thereby corresponding to the usual oven space. This proportion permits good heat distribution into the center of the cooking food. A wide opening at the top of the casserole is desirable for ease of serving and cleaning.

The lid should have a sturdy handle or knob. Side handles to lift the hot dish are common although not

1. The centering movements here are similar to those used in making a plate. The edge of the right hand flattens the top while the curved left hand, pushing inward, centers the side.

2. Now the centered mass is opened and the roll of clay is slowly pulled backward. Pull in one direction. If the clay is tugged laterally, it will be much more apt to spin out of control.

3. Brace your arms tightly against your sides as lifting begins. There must be strong pressure inward to counteract centrifugal force. Avoid leaning on the rim with the left hand.

7. A flanged lid is begun. Here the wall has been lifted diagonally. The left hand lightly steadies the clay while the right hand thickens the rim and keeps it centered.

8. An interior concavity is developed as the wall above it is pulled out more sharply. Too soft a clay or too flat a form may cause the lid to collapse at this point.

9. A critical moment: the form must be right; the lip, kept a double thickness must now be divided; and the flange must be the correct diameter to fit the casserole.

absolutely essential. When pulled handles are used on the sides, they are positioned vertically, as was done here, or horizontally, in which case they may be attached perpendicular or at an angle to the walls of the container. Ledge handles are sometimes made from slabs which have been cut into interesting, decorative shapes. Cylinder handles, or variants of that basic form, are frequently employed and may be seen in the following section on syrup pitchers.

While a flanged lid was used here, other kinds are often chosen, particularly the curved inset lid. Whichever type is wanted, it should be thought of in two ways: as a close-fitting cover and as a form to be related aesthetically to the rest of the container.

4. When possible, the hands are braced together with the thumb. Push in and out to give the form its concave/convex profile. Try for a wall of even thickness from top to bottom.

5. Trim the top level, if this is necessary, before shaping the lip. Shown here being strengthened and refined by the fingertips, the lip should be quite sturdy to support the lid.

6. When the casserole is leather-hard, pulled handles are attached. All surfaces to be joined are scored and slipped. The handle loops should be open enough for the fingers to easily lift the pot.

10. A flexible rib may be used for the finishing trim. Shave carefully where the domed form meets the main curve. Taking the lid up during trimming to test the thickness is good practice.

11. A handle-loop was prepared earlier and is about to be joined to the lid. Regardless of its physical size, a knob or a pulled handle should convince one that it is strong enough to lift the lid.

12. The casserole may receive hard use at the sink and in the stove. Make substantial handles and avoid fragile lips and edges. A little play should be left in the fit of the lid.

SYRUP PITCHER

When one or two pots as small as a syrup pitcher are being thrown, working on the wheelhead is sensible. If more than a few are going to be made, throwing off the hump is worth considering. The "hump" need not be nearly so large as the one shown on page 74.

Although the cylinder handles used here give the small pitchers a distinctive character, pulled handles would serve equally well. Remember that the pouring spout should be eased out to a sharp edge so that syrup will be stopped from trickling down the outside wall.

1. On a form this small using a knuckle for pulling up the clay is usually dispensed with. Once the ball has been opened, lifting and shaping occur almost simultaneously.

2. The spout is shaped by both hands, each playing an essential role. While the right finger eases the clay outward, the left fingers push in and form a channel.

3. Handles of this kind are variants of cylinders and are thrown rather like teapot spouts. Having a group of handles to choose from may yield unexpected combinations of forms.

4. Before deciding on final placement, hold the handle in different positions and at various angles to the pitcher. Trim the handle precisely to conform to the pitcher's curvature.

5. After scoring and slipping the edges, join the parts and work in a small coil around the seam. While drying, the handle may be supported with a lump of clay.

6. The pitcher on the left is for a right-handed person; the one on the right is for a left-hander. Putting two opposite spouts on the same pot will accommodate everyone.

SERVING DISH

This chapter presents some ideas on how wheel forms can be altered and thereby given a different character. It is possible to cut up, batter, and even fondle a pot to the point where it has little, if any, look of the wheel left to it. Using clay in these ways is perfectly valid, and many such pieces have been turned into excellent, highly imaginative forms. The aim here, however, is to suggest several methods of change which, though they carry the piece away from the symmetry associated with the wheel, do not obliterate its traces.

1. Save energy by patting a large mass of clay as nearly on center as possible before spinning the wheel. Body and arms lean into the clay with force. Both hands press to the center.

2. Collaring brings a tapering form in still further. The top must not be permitted to flare out or it will twist and ripple when forced into a small opening.

3. The form is given a further refinement with the aid of a rib, which glides rather lightly, and with a minimum of friction, as clay is pushed against it from the inside.

7. A low, tapering cylinder with heavy walls was thrown to form an open foot. This photograph shows the form leather-hard with one side cut away.

8. Both sides have been removed. When the cylinder was thrown, it was given a bevelled lip which was angled to match the curvature of the serving dish.

9. After its edges were joined, the dish was partially dried upside down. Here, rightside up, smoothed on the interior, and leather-hard, the form rests on its open foot.

The construction of the serving dish illustrates two such methods: first, that parts of wheel-thrown forms may be combined in different contexts (in this case, sections of bowls become handles and a foot); second, that a form may be cut apart and put back together in a different relationship (here, the bell with a vertical axis becomes, when reassembled, a horizontally oriented form).

If he is interested in ideas of change, the potter will begin to take a new view of his wheel forms, perhaps considering ways in which freshly thrown pieces may be modified while the clay is still plastic. He will turn forms upside down and set them on top of one another. He will throw experimental pieces—some simple, some complex—cut them apart, and reassemble the sections in new relationships. Some forms will remain resistant to change while others will lend themselves to modifications that are novel and visually rewarding.

4. The bell-like form is almost complete. Enough clay was left at the top to be curved nearly shut. The finger positions used here are akin to those described when forming a bottle.

5. When firm, the pot was cut from the wheel-head and placed in a chuck—a centered glaze crock. The bottom has been removed with a needle and the inner surface is being smoothed with a metal rib.

6. Sliced vertically into two halves, the pot will soon become a horizontal one. The edges have been bevelled for strength at the joint, then roughened and brushed with slip.

10. A bowl with a finished lip has been thrown to provide handles for the serving dish. The removal of the handles was simplified by cutting out the bottom of the bowl with a needle.

11. The ends of the server were shaved off at an angle to prepare for the handles. These required some flattening at the bottom before attachment to the dish.

12. An attempt was made to keep all elements consistent—the thickness of the walls, the crisp character of the edges, the wheel-look of the parts, etc.—when throwing and assembling the forms.

FLATTENED VASE

The normal cylindricality or round section of a wheel form may be modified or completely changed. Among other possible alterations, the piece can be flattened, paddled squarish, or given a three-sided shape. One part of such a form may have an axis which opposes that of another part—a modification which can most easily be seen by flattening at right angles to each other the top and bottom halves of a tall cylinder.

The most significant alteration to the vase shown here is the one which changed the section from a circle to an

1. In tall cylinders certain maladies become aggravated. Working too long and using too much water will eventually fatigue the form and cause it to slump. Its tendency to flare must be combatted, too.

2. Two different arcs have been cut out of this tongue-depressor which will be used to modify the form. Throwing continues; the clay has not been permitted to harden.

3. The rib is being held tightly against the exterior while the inside fingertips push the clay with considerable force into the concavity.

7. The edges of the outer forms are pushed together, the central space being left open. A coil could be utilized over this space, but a prethrown form will be used instead.

8. A low mass of clay is centered and treated as though a recessed lid were being made. Leaving the middle unworked, the fingertips cut a valley near the outer edge.

9. The center mound has been opened, and a neck is being lifted and shaped. The diameter of the clay at the bat corresponds to the size of the main form's open space.

ellipse. Creasing or grooving the clay may change the form, too, superficially, or, as used here, to create divisions which are sculpturally important yet do not destroy the elliptical form. A rib with a cutout may also effect a change, ranging from one which strongly alters the form to one which modifies the surface. All of the devices mentioned, as well as the use of a preformed top, play an important role in giving the vase its particular quality.

Technically, if a wheel form is to be flattened or paddled to a new shape, it must be caught at the right moment. If too dry it will crack badly; if too wet it will not hold the shape and may collapse. When a form is flattened to the extent shown here, the bottom will split open and must be patched with plastic clay pushed into the crack.

4. The form has been drying for about one hour. Here it is being pressed together with the palms. Plastic clay must be packed into the tear in the floor.

5. Finger grooves clarify the vertical divisions. If the clay wants to crack on the sides while being flattened, a light spray of water may help. Otherwise, the cracks will need to be filled in.

6. The two end forms are trimmed at an angle. Light spraying is a good idea if it seems that thin edges are drying too quickly.

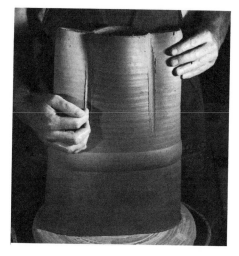

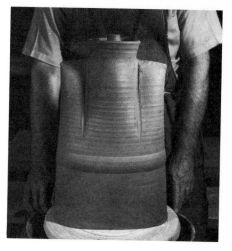

10. Separated from the bat, the form is shown upside down. Since the neck is taller than the wall, trimming is most easily performed by hand with a fettling knife.

11. Both diameters were adjusted to insure an accurate fit. The assembly must be made with care since it will not be possible to work the joint from the inside.

12. The base of the pot was also trimmed with a knife. When the vase was firm, it was set on three dowels to allow even drying around and under the base.

TEAPOT

All thrown forms come from the potter's wheel sharing an inevitable vertical axis. This axial attribute is more apparent in tall cylinders than it is in plates or wide bowls, but it exists in these, too. A pot may be altered, therefore, by tipping the whole form or a part of it and thereby changing its axis.

A teapot ordinarily has several axes, the most important being the vertical one of the pot itself and the diagonal axis of the spout. Three axes, none vertical, are in opposition in this teapot and the form perhaps gains in

1. Shortly after being thrown, the form was paddled and flattened by hand—a treatment which usually tears open the floor. The floor will not be repaired because the entire bottom is to be cut away.

2. The form is pinched in and divided with care being taken to avoid smearing the surface. Cracking will occur at the lip if the clay has become too dry and rigid.

3. The two compartments, each of which was given a round opening, touch only at the top. That joint was pressed together and reinforced. Finger grooves accentuate the division lines.

7. After the assembly, run a small coil around the interior seam and weld it securely. Here a wooden paddle further strengthens the seam and rounds the bottom of the form.

8. The area to which the spout will be attached has been shaved and a tentative cut is being made on the larger form. A sharper slant was later given to the edge.

9. A thin slab has been rolled and cut to fit the spout opening. Strainer holes should be numerous, large in size, and located well inside the outer edges of the slab.

sculptural interest because of these contrasts.

In addition to its axial shifts, the form has been flattened and creased, useful and common methods of change, while the clay is still plastic. Although these treatments alter and reduce its primary wheel character, the teapot nevertheless appears wheelmade. The spout, handle, lid, and finger rings create, or reinforce, this perception, as does the fact that one can look at the pot and see "how it was done."

A technical note: to throw a spout which will fit an oval area, first lay a string around the oval's perimeter; then, open this length of string to a circle and use the circle's diameter when throwing the base of the spout.

4. Standing upright until now, the pot will be tilted by being cut along the scratched line. This will remove the bottom of the form.

5. Pound a lump of clay to flatten it. Then roll a slab, using a level, absorbent surface. Plaster or pressed wood will work well. The thickness can be estimated, or controlled exactly with sticks.

6. A slab 1/4 inch in thickness has been prepared. The contour of the pot will be traced onto the slab which will then be cut to provide a new bottom.

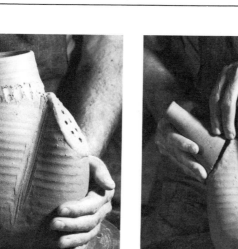

10. A prethrown collar is now set onto the main form and welded into place. Throwing the collar with a coil would have required propping, levelling, and centering the teapot—a finicky, irksome job.

11. With the stainer-slab in place, the spout is tested for the correct angle. The large end of the spout was flattened to conform to the shape of the slab.

12. The spout has been shortened and shaped on the end. A simple flanged lid and a pulled handle—which adds its own ellipse—complete the form.

SQUARED JAR

All potters want to exploit the clay's plasticity, an essential attribute and one that is necessary to effect the change shown on these pages, that of gradually moving the form from a rounded base to a squarish top. The completely flat sides and sharp edges which would have given the jar a cubic, slab-built look were purposely avoided. A more ambiguous and equivocal form was wanted—one which would suggest the pliancy of clay, be soft and cushiony, yet at the same time exhibit elements of angularity and sharpness; one which would

1. When pulling up very thick walls, particularly at the beginning of the lift, the usual knuckle/thumb position may be less effective than the entire fist.

2. A flaring, cylindrical form is being given four equidistant, vertical cuts. Running a piece of string around the lip to find halves and then quarters is an easy way to make such divisions.

3. A V form of about three inches in width is taken out next. This will make it easier to fold the four flaps inward. All of the cuts were made to the same depth.

7. With 1/4 inch of overlap, the edges are slipped and joined. All corners are pinched together and strengthened. Some additional adjustment of the sides develops further the symmetry of the form.

8. After the jar was cut from the wheelhead, the open square at the top was accurately centered. As the wheel spins, a circle for the lid is being removed with a needle.

9. The form has not yet reached the leatherhard stage and is soft enough so that a strip of plywood can easily make impressions on the four sides.

show itself to be clearly derived from the wheel, yet at the same time be unlike anything taken from it.

For its full effect, a form such as this one depends on symmetry, which in turn is dependent on accurate measuring, shaping, and cutting. The four panels should be alike in size and shape (which permits the four decorative impressions to be unvarying). The flaps should be folded carefully to form a square opening. The lid opening, cut with a needle, should be exactly positioned, etc.

A flanged lid, kept simple—without knob or handle—to emphasize its sculptural, geometric nature, completes the jar and relates it again to the wheel.

4. Still rather soft, the piece has set a half-hour after throwing. The four sides are patted lightly with the palms to suggest a squared form.

5. Two opposite sides have been folded inward. The clay must be the right consistency at this time. If too wet, the flaps will not stand; if too dry, the folds will crack.

6. The two remaining flaps are folded over the first pair. Unwanted clay will be trimmed away from each of the eight edges to prevent unnecessarily thick joints.

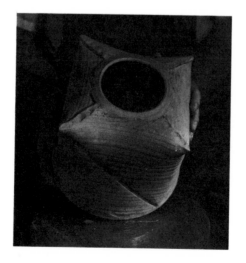

10. A level and strengthened lip will be given to the jar. The coil which is being added to the trimmed edge will be thrown to form a somewhat smaller diameter.

11. This photograph shows the finished lip and the visual relationship of the top to the sides. After the coil was thrown, a measurement was taken for the lid.

12. A flanged lid has been used to cover the jar. Although the lid is too wide to be grasped in one hand, it seemed best to stress simplicity of form rather than attach a knob or a handle.

INVERTED, SQUARED JAR

How does the person using the potter's wheel originate his forms? There are many ways. Some potters take to nature and on walks in the woods find fruits and seedpods whose shapes inspire them. Sketching and doodling works for others, though perhaps more often when one has had experience with clay and knows what to expect from it. A familiarity with historical and contemporary pottery is almost invariably an important stimulus. And it is always exciting to invent or discover forms while actually throwing. With no sketch to guide,

1. The bowl is tested to see if the clay has the proper consistency for cutting and folding. The upper half will be cut into four segments as was the cylinder shown in the previous section.

2. Several steps farther along, the form has been cut and partially flattened. The steps involved in bringing the jar to this point may be seen on the preceding pages.

3. It was not necessary to realign the form as the open square remained on center. The wheel is spinning and a needle trims away a circle to begin the foot of the jar.

7. A second coil was positioned on the slab and lifted into the tall foot shown here. The foot was given a thick wall and a substantial rim to support the jar's considerable weight.

8. While the container was being formed upside down, the plaster bat was helping to dry the upper edge, which is now firm and being roughened with a comb.

9. With the pot on center and the rim slipped, the coil is now welded into place. Clay should be pushed over the joint to seal it both inside and outside.

no mental image of what is wanted, and sometimes not even a thought about function, one can sit at the wheel and on occasion find forms that are fresh and personal.

When one works regularly, not waiting for inspiration to strike, ideas begin to feed on one another. One form suggests two or three others. Making a series of similar pots, each one slightly varied, is a useful method and can lead to expressive forms (and an increasing ability to recognize them) which might not be arrived at in any other way.

The jar pictured here is one of a series. An upside-down variant of the container shown in the preceding section, it dramatizes transition and change even more strongly than did that one—in this case the transition from a squared center to the circular, wheel forms of top and bottom.

4. The circle does not lie on one plane, being higher where it crosses the four seams. To overcome this condition, a transitional form is being thrown from a coil.

5. After the form was completed, the diameter of the opening was taken. On a rolled slab that measurement is used to prepare a bottom for the jar.

6. When both forms were leather-hard, the slab was slipped and joined to the rim. This illustration shows the slab being trimmed around the edges.

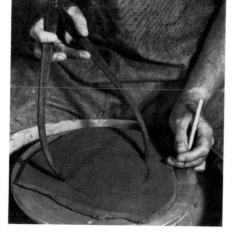

10. An ample amount of clay was required to conclude the form. After being centered, the coil was divided into an inner ledge and a flaring lip according to the method explained on pages 44–45.

11. A pulled handle, a weightier visual form than a normal-sized knob, was decided on and is shown being attached to a flat lid when both are of a similar consistency.

12. To minimize warpage, the lid is customarily fired on the jar. They may come from the kiln stuck together superficially. A flared lip rather than a vertical one allows a knife tip to separate them.

JAR WITH CUT HANDLES

Of the many possibilities which exist for modifying wheelforms, some of the most interesting and least tried grow, literally and figuratively, out of the manner in which thrown coils may be employed.

Setting a coil directly on the rim of the pot can, as has been illustrated, provide extra clay to increase its height and bring the form to conclusion. Or, placing a coil on a trimmed, inverted bowl enables one to throw a foot and make a goblet or a compote.

A different way to use a coil is to throw it from the wall

1. Centering a large piece of clay can be wearying. Before spinning the wheel and using any water, paddle the mass vigorously into a hemispherical form.

2. A good deal of force is needed to drive a hole into this amount of clay. Use all the fingers, holding them tightly together in a wedgelike form, and burrow into the mass. Brace the arms against the body.

3. A tightened fist will provide the necessary strength to pull up an extra-thick wall. Undercut the clay strongly on the inside to get beneath the mass and start it moving.

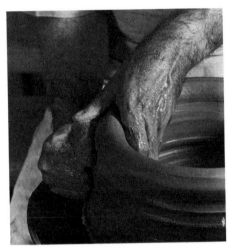

7. Before throwing a coil, take the time to push clay over the joint, both inside and outside. Hold a fingernail against the spinning coil to see if it is on center; adjust it if necessary.

8. A sponge keeps the surface moist while the coil is lifted. To avoid getting the trough too wet, slip rather than water is used to lubricate the clay.

9. Collaring steadies the rim, reduces the diameter of the opening, and provides a final thickness of clay to form a shoulder for the lid.

of a leather-hard form. Either the outside or the inside wall (as was the case here) may be utilized. If thrown on the inside wall, the coil can be lifted to a form which terminates the pot while the primary edges remain to be used as one wishes—in this example as handles. A single coil or many may be thrown from an exterior wall. When attached to a vertical surface, a coil may be thrown horizontally (to a length of several inches), diagonally, or into a curve. A single flange or a series (parallel to or opposing one another) may be left as thrown, or

bent, or cut in ways which will strongly affect the sculptural quality or the surface of the form.

Good judgment must be shown regarding the placement and weight of any coil which is to be thrown. A heavy coil placed on a sweeping curve or an abnormally thin wall would be most apt to deform it then or during firing.

4. Close to its final height, the cylinder is given a concave form with the aid of a rib. The fingertips inside are pressing opposite the spot where the wood touches the clay.

5. The preceding photograph shows that extra clay was left at the top of the cylinder. Here it is being utilized to give a wide, almost horizontal flare to the form.

6. The jar has dried awhile. From thoroughly wedged clay a thick coil has been rolled and is being placed inside the pot along the line where the plane changes direction.

10. Cutting and carving, as well as trimming, are most easily done at the leather-hard stage. Four arcs are now cut from the flange to form the handles.

11. Very infrequently does one form represent the only possible solution, the inevitable, "right" answer. This jar might be covered interestingly by a variety of lids. Two possibilities are shown.

12. Sketching a form and its components may suggest alternative solutions. Actually making the components lets one experience the difference in ways that could not be anticipated on paper.

APPENDIX

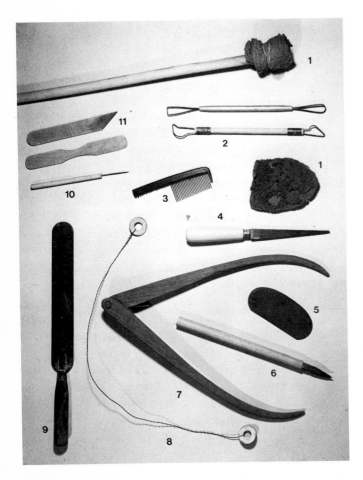

Tools. Those most frequently used throughout this book are pictured above.

1. Sponges are used to moisten clay, refine edges, and remove excess water from the interior of pots.
2. Trimming tools, with wire or loop ends, are used to trim pots at the leather-hard stage.
3. A comb can roughen a clay surface in preparation for attaching a coil, handle, or knob.
4. The fettling knife trims pots and clay slabs.
5. A flexible metal rib is used to help shape curves and to trim and scrape surfaces.
6. A Japanese brush applies clay slip to scored surfaces which are to be joined.

7. The calipers take measurements for lids and of forms which are to be similar in size.
8. A cut-off wire, formed of two twisted strands, cuts a pot from the wheelhead or bat.
9. The spatula affords one means of cutting a small form—a cup or a lid—from the hump.
10. A needle is used to trim the lip during throwing and to gauge the thickness of the clay floor.
11. Tongue depressors assist in throwing, trim excess clay, and form decorative bands.

Clay. A full discussion of clays is beyond the scope of this book. For that information the student is advised to read a basic text such as *Clay and Glazes for the Potter* by Daniel Rhodes. What follows is written to assist the person who wishes to buy his clay and/or prepare his own clay body. It would be helpful, first of all, to talk to a studio potter, a teacher, or a supplier about clays and particularly about those that are available in your area.

You will want to select a clay whose firing range can be accommodated in the kiln you are using. Low-firing clays—those in the earthenware group—fire in a range from approximately 1,800°F to somewhat beyond 2,000°F. Stoneware clays mature at higher temperatures and vitrify (harden and glassify) when fired in a range from 2,150°F to 2,380°F. Porcelains, clay mixtures which fire white and translucent, usually require a temperature in excess of 2,300°F.

Clays are in abundance in nature and may be found along river banks, in fields, at the site of excavations, etc. If you go prospecting and a deposit is located, the clay will almost certainly need preparation. Pulverizing dry lumps and soaking and sieving to remove rocks and leaves are a part of the necessary conditioning process. Later, the clay will need to be tested thoroughly as regards plasticity, drying characteristics, shrinkage, and absorption. You must then decide whether the effort needed to dig and prepare a clay is offset by its quality and the savings effected.

Most potters choose to purchase their clay, either dry or in plastic form. Although cheaper if bought dry, clay must then be mixed with water to the desired consistency. When buying a clay, one may be getting a single variety or a clay body—a mixture of clays and nonplastic additives such as flint, feldspar, and grog.

A more experienced potter may decide to formulate and mix a clay body to his own specifications. Although there is no guaranteed way to begin, try starting with a familiar clay—one which approaches your requirements as nearly as possible. Here are some ways in which a basic stoneware clay may be modified if improvement in its performance is considered necessary. The addition of 10 to 30 percent of ball clay will improve plasticity as well as increase the shrinkage rate. A 10 to 25 percent addition of red earthenware clay will lower the maturing point, darken the color, and usually improve plasticity. By adding 10 to 40 percent of fire clay, the maturing point will be raised, the plasticity reduced, a coarser texture or "tooth" added, and drying characteristics improved.

The nonplastic additives are often valuable components of a clay body, while having the disadvantage of reducing plasticity when used excessively. Flint will contribute hardness and increase the maturing point. Feldspar reduces the maturing point and promotes vitrification. Grog (a fired, crushed clay) will, in adding tooth, promote even drying and lessen shrinkage.

A potter who has gone to the trouble of devising and testing a clay body will probably want to use large amounts of it. A studio clay mixer will facilitate the preparation of one's blend, having the capacity to mix several hundred pounds in an hour. If you have neither the space for a clay mixer nor the money to invest in such a machine, consider taking your formula to a commercial supplier. Many supply houses will mix your personal blend if you are willing to purchase the body by the ton.

Shrinkage. Clay shrinks during drying because the water, which was used to make it plastic, has evaporated. One important consequence is that clay parts which are of very different water content cannot be joined successfully. For example, in making a compote (page 61), if the bowl is completely dry it will have undergone considerable shrinkage. When a moist or leather-hard foot is attached to it, the foot will eventually shrink and crack apart. Attaching a dry foot to a wet bowl produces the same result. It is essential, therefore, that components be attached when they are of a similar consistency.

Shrinkage Test. Shrinkage continues during firing as vitrification occurs. It is frequently useful to know exactly how much one's clay will shrink from the time it is plastic until it has been fired. One may, for example, want a cup or a bowl to be a specific size after firing. If the percentage of shrinkage is known, the piece can be made proportionately larger. To find the total shrinkage, take a lump of clay of the consistency you customarily use. Very moist clay will shrink more than stiffer, drier clay. Roll a slab to a thickness of ¼ inch. From it cut a rectangular tile 2 by 5 inches or 4 by 12 cm. Lay a metric ruler on the tile and mark off a line 100 mm. in length. To prevent warping, dry the tile carefully between plaster bats. When the tile has dried completely (the clay is now referred to as bone dry), fire it unglazed. Subtracting the line's final metric length in millimeters (after firing) from 100 will give the percentage of linear shrinkage from the plastic to the fired state.

Absorption Test. A fired, unglazed sample of one's clay is weighed, soaked in water overnight, wiped off, and weighed again. The absorption of the clay is determined by calculating the percentage of gain in weight. Average absorption ranges are as follows: earthenware, 3 to 10 percent; stoneware, 1 to 5 percent; porcelain, 0 to 3 percent. If the clay absorbs water excessively, it will be soft and porous. Adding feldspar or another flux will help to eliminate the problem.

Preparing Plaster. A knowledge of this material will enable one to make molds, a wedging board, plaster bats, and decorating stamps. Bats can be formed one at a time, or several can be made at the same pouring almost as easily. A medium-sized dishpan is large enough to make two bats. For each bat, fill a pie or pizza tin with water and then pour the water into the dishpan. Coat the interior of the pie tin with liquid soap, shortening, etc. Such a coating will allow the hardened plaster to separate more easily.

Lightly and evenly sprinkle pottery or moulding plaster onto the water, continuing until the water has absorbed all the plaster it can hold. At that point a thin dusting of plaster will begin to lie on the surface. Then, and not before, put your hand beneath the water and gently agitate the mixture, breaking the lumps with your fingers. Pour the plaster into the pie tin almost to overflowing. Unused plaster from the dishpan should be removed and discarded rather than washed down the sink. When the plaster has partially hardened, take a metal or hardwood straightedge and scrape across the rim of the pie tin to remove the excess. This will insure that the top and bottom surfaces of the bat are parallel. After the plaster has completely hardened, tap the rim to release the bat. Allow the bat to dry thoroughly before using it.

Wheels. The potter's wheels shown here, which constitute a representative though by no means complete listing, vary in cost, design, and performance characteristics. Three groups exist. The most basic is the kick wheel which is usually operated by foot power although a motor may be attached to it. One kicks a heavy flywheel made of metal, concrete, or weighted wood, and the motion is transmitted to a wheelhead. It is a simple, relatively inexpensive mechanism which permits exact control of the speed. It may be purchased assembled or in kit form. If one builds a wooden frame around the running parts, attention should be given to comfortably-positioned footrests and the placement of the seat.

Foot power is also required to operate the treadle wheel. One must develop the coordination to keep a treadle moving constantly, from a standing or seated position, while at the same time maintaining the steadiness needed to control the clay and form a pot.

Although an electric wheel may be quite expensive (cheap models of superior quality are nonexistent), it

1. Klopfenstein treadle wheel, 30″ × 30″ × 5″. 14 ga. rustproofed steel pan. 13″ wheelhead. 100 lb., 20″ flywheel. Trim bar for foot rimming. Height 36″. Hip rest (nonadjustable). Reversible throwing head optional.

2. Carlos Frey kickwheel. 1/2 hp motor attachment optional. Adjustable seat, countertop, flywheel, and footrests. 180 lb. reinforced concrete flywheel. 13″ wheelhead. Total wheel weight 260 lbs. Disassembles completely.

3. Robert Brent electric wheel. Two piece splash pan. Foot pedal can be used on either side. Adjustable seat. 12″ or 14″ aluminum wheelhead. Shown with optional leg extensions. Other options include 1/3, 1/2, or 1 hp AC motor.

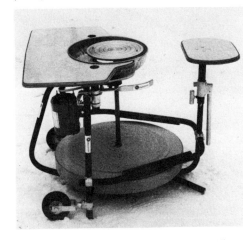

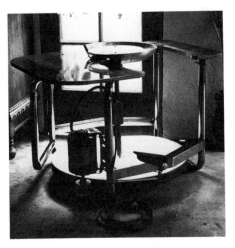
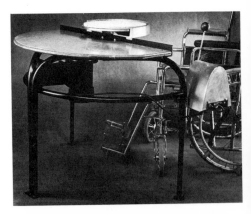

7. Creative Industries electric wheel. Foot pedal can be positioned anywhere. Wheelhead speed remains constant when foot leaves pedal. 18″ × 24″ tabletop. Options include 1/3 or 1 1/3 hp (0-220 rpm), 12″ or 14″ wheelhead, splashpan.

8. Conway kickwheel. Adjustable seat. 130 lb. flywheel. Cast aluminum splashpan and wheelhead. 1/2 or 3/4 hp motor attachment optional. Variable speed control to 180 rpm. Control pedal on the footrest.

9. Soldner "handicapped wheel." 1/4 hp motor, variable speed. 14″ cast aluminum wheelhead. Adjustable height. Speed controlled by hand or foot. Although built for a person in a wheelchair, the wheel can be used in the usual way.

can be a good investment because of its advantages. Compact and portable, it will nonetheless handle a huge amount of clay if the motor has sufficient torque and horsepower. To have the necessary degree of control, one should choose a model with variable speeds and an appropriate rpm range of 0–150. The electric wheel is an undoubted energy-saver, particularly if one intends to work long periods in the studio. When kits are available, substantial savings may be possible.

1. *H. B. Klopfenstein & Sons, Route Two, Crestline, Ohio 44827*
2. *Mid-America Art Studio, 7th & Logan, Wayne, Nebr. 68787*
3. *Robert Brent Co., 128 Mill St., Healdsburg, Calif. 95448*
4. *Cutter Ceramics, 47 Athletic Field Road, Waltham, Mass. 02154*
5. *Thomas Stuart Kick Wheels, P.O. Box 9699, Denver, Colo. 80223*
6. *Shimpo-West, P.O. Box 2315, La Puente, Calif. 91746*
7. *Creative Industries, P.O. Box 343, La Mesa, Calif. 92041*
8. *Conway Wheels, P.O. Box 4032, Boulder, Colo. 80302*
9. *Soldner Pottery Equipment, Inc., P.O. Box 428, Silt, Colo. 81652*
10. *A. D. Alpine, Inc., 3051 Fujita St., Torrance, Calif. 90505*
11. *Randall Potters, Inc., Box 774, Alfred, N.Y. 14802*
12. *Menco Engineers, Inc., 5520 Crebs Ave., Tarzana, Calif. 91356*

4. Cutter kickwheel. Fir, spruce, and plywood frame. 150 lb. reinforced concrete flywheel. Adjustable seat, 12″ aluminum wheelhead. Fiberglass splashpan optional. A kit of the metal parts is available.

5. Thomas Stuart kickwheel. Adjustable seat and footrests. 140 lb. reinforced concrete flywheel. Galvanized steel pipe construction. Disassembles completely. Options include aluminum splashpan and motor attachment.

6. Shimpo-West electric wheel. 1/4 hp motor. Variable speeds, 20-220 rpm. Speed adjustable by foot or hand. Operating switch reverses wheelhead direction. Adjustable legs. Molded plastic splashpan with attached shelf.

10. Alpine kickwheel. 1/2 hp motor attachment available. 150 lb. metal flywheel. 13″ cast aluminum wheelhead. Aluminum splashpan optional. Adjustable seat. Leveling bolts on all legs. 2″ steel pipe frame.

11. Randall electric wheel. High torque, variable speed, 3/4 hp motor. Shown with 18″ aluminum flat head for large pots or wide plates. Other options available include: 14″ wheelhead, bucket head for plaster bats, splash pan.

12. Spinning Tiger electric wheel 0-240 rpm. Infinitely variable speed. 12″ aluminum wheelhead. Options available include: 1/3 hp DC motor or 1/2 hp permanent magnet motor, splash pan and stand.

INDEX